Presented to:

_____

By:

_____

Date:

_____

Chariot Books™ is an imprint of David C. Cook Publishing Co.
David C. Cook Publishing Co., Elgin, Illinois 60120
David C. Cook Publishing Co., Weston, Ontario
Kingsway Communications UK, Eastbourne, England

THE KID-BUILDER BIBLE
© 1994 by David C. Cook Publishing Co. for text and Bible art illustrations.

Illustrations by David Barnett
Cover design by Larry Taylor Design
Internal design by Nancy L. Haskins
Edited by Linda Washington

Scripture taken from the Holy Bible, New Life Version, Copyright © *1969, 1987, 1993 by Christian Literature International, P.O. Box 777, Canby, OR 97013*
Editions of the complete New Life Version are distributed to the trade by Victor Books.

First Printing, 1994
Printed in the United States of America
98 97 96 95 94   5 4 3 2 1

Library of Congress Cataloging-in-Publication Data

Bible. English. New Life. Selections. 1994
    The kid-builder Bible ; New Life Version.
    p.   cm.
    ISBN 0-7814--0075-9
    [1. Bible Stories.]   I. Chariot Books   II. Title.
BS391.2.C436 1994
220.5'208--dc20

                                                                94-11889
                                                                    CIP
                                                                    AC

THE KID-BUILDER BIBLE

For Young Readers

Chariot Books™
A Division of Cook Communications

Bible Book Abbreviations

Here is a chart to help you know how each book name is abbreviated in your Kid-Builder Bible.

Old Testament

Genesis	Gen.
Exodus	Exod.
Leviticus	Lev.
Numbers	Num.
Deuteronomy	Deut.
Joshua	Josh.
Judges	Judg.
Ruth	Ruth
I Samuel	I Sam.
II Samuel	II Sam.
I Kings	I Kings
II Kings	II Kings
I Chronicles	I Chron.
II Chronicles	II Chron.
Ezra	Ezra
Nehemiah	Neh.
Esther	Esth.
Job	Job
Psalms	Ps.
Proverbs	Prov.
Ecclesiastes	Eccl.
Song of Solomon	Song of Sol.
Isaiah	Isa.
Jeremiah	Jer.
Lamentations	Lam.
Ezekiel	Ezek.
Daniel	Dan.
Hosea	Hos.
Joel	Joel
Amos	Amos
Obadiah	Obad.
Jonah	Jonah
Micah	Mic.
Nahum	Nah.
Habakkuk	Hab.
Zephaniah	Zeph.
Haggai	Hag.
Zechariah	Zech.
Malachi	Mal.

New Testament

Matthew	Matt.
Mark	Mark
Luke	Luke
John	John
Acts	Acts
Romans	Rom.
I Corinthians	I Cor.
II Corinthians	II Cor.
Galatians	Gal.
Ephesians	Eph.
Philippians	Phil.
Colossians	Col.
I Thessalonians	I Thes.
II Thessalonians	II Thes.
I Timothy	I Tim.
II Timothy	II Tim.
Titus	Titus
Philemon	Philem.
Hebrews	Heb.
James	Jas.
I Peter	I Pet.
II Peter	II Pet.
I John	I John
II John	II John
III John	III John
Jude	Jude
Revelation	Rev.

Kids, . . .
A Bible That is
Fun to Read!

The Kid-Builder Bible will help you enjoy reading God's Word. It takes a giant step from the Bible storybooks you've looked at in the past to actual Bible passages that you can read yourself. *The Kid-Builder Bible* is easy-to-read and easy-to-understand, written for kids like you.

Every selection has been specially chosen to show you how exciting the Bible really is. As you read, you will see stories about real people who trusted in God. You'll also find Scripture passages that help when times get tough, times when you need to know that God is there for you.

Other exciting features to look for are:

• Colorful pictures to make the Bible come alive!

• Short verses to memorize!

• Prayers to get you started talking to God!

• Pointers on *how to* and *how not to* pray!

• Background information on every book!

• Questions to help you think about how God's truths can work in your everyday situation!

The most important thing is to spend time reading God's Word, and with *The Kid-Builder Bible*, reading God's Word yourself will always be fun!

TABLE OF CONTENTS

THE OLD TESTAMENT

I and II Samuel

I and II Kings/I and II Chronicles

Ezra, Nehemiah, and Esther

Poetry and Wisdom

Job, Psalms, Proverbs, Ecclesiastes, Song of Solomon

The Prophets

Isaiah, Jeremiah, Lamentations, Ezekiel, Daniel, Hosea, Joel, Amos, Obadiah, Jonah, Micah, Nahum, Habakkuk, Zephaniah, Haggai, Zechariah, Malachi

THE NEW TESTAMENT

Acts of the Apostles

The Letters

Romans, I/II Corinthians, Galatians, Ephesians, Philippians, Colossians, I/II Thessalonians, I/II Timothy, Titus, Philemon, Hebrews, James, I/II Peter, I/II/III John, and Jude

The Revelation to John

Revelation

Old Testament

THE *Old Testament* has thirty-nine books. It is the largest section of the Bible. Its books cover the time of Creation until about 400 B.C., the time of Ezra and Nehemiah. Books range from Genesis through Malachi. The word *testament* means covenant or agreement. Throughout the Old Testament, stories of God's chosen people, the Israelites, shape God's covenant with man. The story of man's beginning, history of the people of Israel, and prophecies of the coming Messiah are just a few of the events described in these books.

The *Old Testament* is divided into sections, like a library. Each section has a specific type of book. The books of *Creation and the Law* are in the first section. These books tell how God created all things and gave His people laws to guide their lives. The books of *Old Testament History* make up the second section. They give the history of the nation of Israel from the time of their arrival into the promised land of Canaan, through their captivity in foreign lands hundreds of years later. The books of *Poetry and Wisdom* make up the third section. They are filled with wise sayings. *The Prophets* is the last section. These books were written by men chosen by God to give His message to His people.

THE LAW

Creation and the Law

The first five books of the Old Testament are known as the *Law*. These books include Genesis, Exodus, Leviticus, Numbers, and Deuteronomy—all written by Moses. He wrote about how Hebrews were to eat, dress, build houses, and worship. All the Jewish laws, rules, and customs appear in these books. They also highlight the beginnings of the nation of Israel, their years of slavery in Egypt, and their forty-year journey from Egypt to the promised land of Canaan.

Genesis

Genesis (JEN-uh-sis) means "beginning" and is the title of the first book of the Bible. It is a book about beginnings. It tells how God created the world and people. It tells about the beginning of sin, the beginning of God's judgment of sin, and God's compassion for sinners. It also tells about the beginning of the Jewish people.

The Creation

Genesis 1—2

In the beginning God made from nothing the heavens and the earth. ²The earth was an empty waste and darkness was over the deep waters. . . . ³Then God said, "Let there be light," and there was light. ⁴God saw that the light was good. He divided the light from the darkness. ⁵Then God called the light day, and He called the darkness night. There was evening and there was morning, one day.

⁶Then God said, "Let there be an open space between the waters. Let it divide waters from waters." ⁷God made the open space, and divided the waters under the open space from the waters above the open space. And it was so. ⁸Then God called the open space Heaven. There was evening and there was morning, the second day.

⁹Then God said, "Let the waters under the heavens be gathered into one place. Let the dry land be seen." And it was so. ¹⁰Then God called the dry land Earth. He called the gathering of the waters Seas. And God saw that it was good. ¹¹Then God

said, "Let plants grow from the earth, plants that have seeds. Let fruit trees grow on the earth . . ." And it was so. ¹². . . And God saw that it was good. ¹³There was evening and there was morning, the third day.

¹⁴Then God said, "Let there be lights in the open space of the heavens to divide day from night. Let them tell the days and years and times of the year." ¹⁵. . . And it was so. ¹⁶Then God made the two great lights, the brighter light to rule the day, and the smaller light to rule the night. He made the stars also . . . ¹⁸And God saw that it was good. ¹⁹There was evening and there was morning, the fourth day.

²⁰Then God said, "Let the waters be full of living things. Let birds fly above the earth in the open space of the heavens." ²¹God made the big animals that live in the sea, and every living thing that moves through the waters by its kind, and every winged bird after its kind. And God saw that it was good . . . ²³There was evening and there was morning, the fifth day. . . .

²⁵Then God made the wild animals of the earth

Kid-Builder Fact
Gen. 2:3 Before God made light, everything was in darkness. On the first day of creation, God made light. This light did not come from the sun, moon, and stars, or from electricity. The brightness of this light was created by God who separated it from darkness. God called it *day*.

after their kind, and the cattle after their kind, and every thing that moves upon the ground after its kind. And God saw that it was good.

²⁶Then God said, "Let Us make man like Us and let him be head over the fish of the sea, and over the birds of the air, and over . . . every thing that moves on the ground." ²⁷And God made man in His own likeness. . . . ³¹God saw all that He had made and it was very good. There was evening and there was morning, the sixth day.

²:¹So the heavens and the earth were completed, and all that is in them. ²On the seventh day God ended His work which He had done. . . . Then God honored the seventh day and made it holy, because in it He rested from all His work which He had done. . . .

⁶A fog came from the earth and watered the whole top of the ground. ⁷Then the Lord God made man from the dust of the ground. And He breathed into his nose the breath of life. Man became a living being. ⁸The Lord God planted a garden to the east in Eden. He put the man there whom He had made. ⁹And the Lord God made to grow out of the ground every tree that is pleasing to the eyes and good for food. And He made the tree of life grow in the center of the garden, and the tree of learning of good and bad. . . .

¹⁵Then the Lord took the man and put him in the garden of Eden to work the ground and care for it.

¹⁶The Lord God told the man, "You are free to eat from any tree of the garden. ¹⁷But do not eat from the tree of learning of good and bad. For the day you eat from it you will die for sure."

¹⁸Then the Lord God said, "It is not good for man to be alone. I will make a helper that is right for him." ¹⁹Out of the ground the Lord God made every animal of the field and every bird of the sky. He brought them to the man to find out what he would call them. And whatever the man called a living thing, that was its name. ²⁰Adam gave names to all the cattle, and to the birds of the sky, and to every animal of the field. But there was no helper found that was right for Adam. ²¹So the Lord God put the man to sleep. . . . And while he was sleeping, He took one of the bones from his side and closed up the place with flesh. ²²The Lord God made woman from the bone which He had taken from the man. And He brought her to the man. ²³The man said, "This is now bone of my bones, and flesh of my flesh. She will be called Woman, because she was taken out of Man." . . . ²⁵The man and his wife were both without clothes and were not ashamed."

Kid-Builder Value
WORSHIP means to honor and adore someone who is worthy of such high honor. God deserves to be worshiped. Only He could have created the world and everything in it.

KID-BUILDER Questions

- Genesis 3:20 tells us that Adam named his wife Eve. What else did Adam name?

- How do you think God felt when He was all finished making His creation? How do you feel after you've worked hard to make something?

- Why do you think God deserves to be worshiped?

KID-BUILDER Prayer

Lord, You created everything! You deserve to be worshiped! Help me to give honor to Your name.
In Jesus' name. Amen.

Memory Verse:
Give to the Lord the honor that belongs to Him. Worship the Lord in the beauty of holy living.
Ps. 29:2

GENESIS

Man Does Not Obey God

Genesis 3

Now the snake was more able to fool others than any animal of the field which the Lord God had made. He said to the woman, "Did God say that you should not eat from any tree in the garden?" . . .

The woman said to the snake, "We may eat the fruit of the trees of the garden. 3But from the tree which is in the center of the garden, God has said, 'Do not eat from it or touch it, or you will die.' "

4The snake said to the woman, "No, you for sure will not die! 5For God knows that when you eat from it, your eyes will be opened and you will be like God, knowing good and bad." 6The woman saw that the tree was good for food, and pleasing to the eyes, and could fill the desire of making one wise. So she took of its fruit and ate. She also gave some to her husband, and he ate. 7Then the eyes of both of them were opened, and they knew they were without clothes. So they sewed fig leaves together and made themselves clothing.

⁸Then they heard the sound of the Lord God walking in the garden in the evening. The man and his wife hid themselves from the Lord God among the trees of the garden. . . .⁹The Lord God called to the man. He said to him, "Where are you?". . . ¹⁰The man said, "I heard the sound of You in the garden. I was afraid because I was without clothes. So I hid myself." ¹¹The Lord God said, "Who told you that you were without clothes? Have you eaten from the tree of which I told you not to eat?" ¹²The man said, "The woman whom You gave to be with me, she gave me fruit of the tree, and I ate." ¹³Then the Lord God said to the woman, "What is this you have done?" The woman said, "The snake fooled me, and I ate."

¹⁴Then the Lord God said to the snake, "Because you have done this, you will be hated and will suffer more than all cattle, and more than every animal of the field. You will go on your stomach and you will eat dust all the days of your life. ¹⁵And I

will make you and the woman hate each other, and your seed and her seed will hate each other. He will crush your head, and you will crush his heel."

16To the woman He said, ". . . You will give birth to children in pain. . . . Your desire will be for your husband, and he will rule over you."

17Then He said to Adam, "Because you have listened to . . . your wife, and have eaten from the tree of which I told you, 'Do not eat from it,' the ground is cursed because of you. By hard work you will eat food from it all the days of your life. 18It will grow thorns and thistles for you. . . .19You will eat bread by the sweat of your face because of hard work, until you return to the ground, because you were taken from the ground. You are dust, and you will return to dust."

20The man called his wife's name Eve, because she was the mother of all living. 21The Lord God made clothes of skins for Adam and his wife, and dressed them. . . .

23The Lord God sent him out from the garden of Eden, to work the ground from which he was taken. 24So He drove the man out. And He placed cherubim east of the garden of Eden with a sword of fire that turned every way. They kept watch over the path to the tree of life.

Kid-Builder Value
OBEDIENCE is doing what you're instructed to do.
Adam and Eve disobeyed God when they ate from the tree.

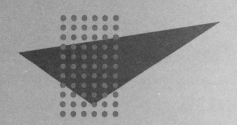

KID-BUILDER Questions

- Read Genesis 2:16, 17. What was God's command? How did Adam and Eve disobey?

- How do you feel after you have done something wrong?

- What are some rules your parents have? What happens when you don't obey their rules?

KID-BUILDER Prayer

Lord, I don't always do what I should. I'm sorry for the wrong things I have done. Please forgive me. Help me to forgive others.   In Jesus' name. Amen.

Memory Verse:
Love the Lord your God. Always do what He tells you and keep all His Laws.   Deut. 11:1

• •

GENESIS

Noah and the Flood

Genesis 6—9

This is the story of Noah and his family. Noah was right with God. . . . ¹⁰And Noah became the father of three sons: Shem, Ham, and Japheth. ¹¹Now the earth was sinful in the eyes of God. The earth was filled with people hurting each other. ¹²God looked at the earth and saw how sinful it was. . . .

¹³Then God said to Noah, "I have decided to make an end to all the people on the earth. . . . See, I will destroy them as I destroy the earth. ¹⁴Make a large boat of gopher wood for yourself. Build rooms in the boat. And cover it inside and out with tar. . . .The boat is to be as long as 150 long steps, as wide as twenty-five long steps, and eight times taller than a man. ¹⁶Make a window for the boat, that goes down an arm's length from the roof. Put a door in the side of the boat. And make it with first, second, and third floors. ¹⁷"See, I will bring a flood of water upon the earth, to destroy all flesh under heaven that has the breath of life.

Everything on earth will be destroyed. ¹⁸But I will make My agreement with you. You will go into the large boat, you and your sons and your wife, and your sons' wives with you. ¹⁹You are to bring into the large boat two of every kind of living thing of all flesh, to keep them alive with you. They will be male and female. ²⁰Two of all the kinds of birds, and animals, and every thing that moves on the ground are to be with you to keep them alive. ²¹And take with you every kind of food that is eaten, and store it. It will be food for you and for them." ²²Noah did just what God told him to do. . . .

⁷:¹⁷The flood came upon the earth for forty days. The water got deeper . . . until all the high mountains under heaven were covered. . . . ²¹All flesh that moved on the earth was destroyed, birds and cattle and wild animals, and every man. . . . ²³God destroyed every living thing upon the land. . . . Only Noah was left, and those that were with him in the large boat. ²⁴And the water covered the earth for 150 days. . . .

⁸:⁴In the seventh month, on the seventeenth day of the month, the large boat came to rest on Mount Ararat. . . .

Kid-Builder Fact

Gen. 8:20 An *altar* is a structure made of stone, wood, marble, brick, or other materials; it is used in worship. Altars were common in pagan religions as well as Judaism. Some altars were very simple; others were fancy.

13In the year 601, in the first month, on the first day of the month, the water was dried up from the earth. Then Noah took the covering off the large boat, and looked out and saw that the earth was dry. . . . 15Then God said to Noah, 16"Go out of the boat, you and your wife and your sons and your sons' wives with you. 17Bring out with you every living thing of all flesh that is with you, birds and animals and everything that moves on the earth." 18So Noah went out with his sons and his wife and his sons' wives. 19Every animal, every bird, . . . went out of the large boat by their families.

20Then Noah built an altar to the Lord. He took of every clean animal and every clean bird, and gave burnt gifts in worship on the altar.

9:8Then God said to Noah . . . 11"I make My agreement with you, that never again will all flesh be destroyed by the water of a flood. . . . 13I will set My rain-bow in the cloud. . . . 16When the rain-bow is in the cloud, I will look upon it to remember the agreement that will last forever between God and every living thing of all flesh that is on the earth."

Kid-Builder Value
FAITHFULNESS means being loyal or full of faith. It is a measure of your relationship to God. It is also a characteristic of God. Because Noah was faithful to God, he and his family were saved from the Flood.

KID-BUILDER Questions

- How did God save Noah and his family from the Flood?

- What was God's promised sign of faithfulness to Noah?

- What do you think it means to be faithful to God?

- In what ways could someone say you are faithful?

KID-BUILDER Prayer

Lord, thank You for teaching me the lesson of being faithful like Noah. Help me to be persistent in faithfulness.   *In Jesus' name. Amen.*

Memory Verse:
[The Lord's] loving-pity never ends. It is new every morning. He is so very faithful.   Lam. 3:22b, 23

GENESIS

God Keeps His Promise

Genesis 17, 18, 21

Abram was a man of faith who went wherever God told him to go. Abram and his wife, Sarai, could not have children. The Lord had promised to give them a child. Abram and Sarai's maid Hagar had a child named Ishmael. But Ishmael was not the promised child.

When Abram was ninety-nine years old, the Lord came to him and said, "I am God All-powerful. . . . ²I will keep My agreement between Me and you. I will give you many children." ³Then Abram fell on his face. God said to him, ". . . You will be the father of many nations. ⁵No more will your name be Abram. But your name will be Abraham. For I will make you the father of many nations. ⁶Many will come from you. . . . Kings will come from you. . . . As for Sarai your wife, do not call her name Sarai. But Sarah will be her name. ¹⁶And I will bring good to her. I will give you a son by her. . . . And she will be the mother of nations.

Kings of many people will come from her."

17Then Abraham fell on his face and laughed. He said to himself, "Will a child be born to a man who is 100 years old?" 18Then Abraham said to God, "If only Ishmael might live before You!" 19But God said, "No, but your wife Sarah will give birth to your son. And you will give him the name Isaac. I will make My agreement with him and for his children after him, an agreement that will last forever. . . . 21I will make My agreement with Isaac, who will be born to Sarah at this time next year.". . .

18:1The Lord showed Himself to Abraham by the oak trees of Mamre, as he sat at the tent door in the heat of the day. 2Abraham looked up and saw three men standing in front of him. When he saw them, he ran from the tent door to meet them. He put his face to the ground 3and said, "My lord, if I have found favor in your eyes, please do not pass by your servant. 4Let us have a little water brought to wash your feet. Rest yourselves under the tree. 5And I will get a piece of bread so you may eat and get strength. . . ."

The men said, "Do as you have said." 6So Abraham ran into the tent to Sarah, and said, "Hurry and get three pails of fine flour, mix it well, and make bread." 7Then Abraham ran to the cattle and took out a young and good calf. He gave it to the servant to make it ready in a hurry. 8He took milk and cheese and the meat which he had made ready, and set it in front of them. He stood by them under the tree while they ate.

⁹Then they said to him, "Where is your wife Sarah?" And he said, "There in the tent." ¹⁰The Lord said, "I will be sure to return to you at this time next year. And your wife Sarah will have a son." Sarah was listening at the tent door behind him. ¹¹Now Abraham and Sarah were old. They had lived many years. . . . ¹²So Sarah laughed to herself, saying, "Will I have this joy after my husband and I have grown old?" ¹³Then the Lord said to Abraham, "Why did Sarah laugh and say, 'How can I give birth to a child when I am so old?' ¹⁴Is anything too hard for the Lord? I will return to you at this time next year, and Sarah will have a son.". . .

²¹:¹Then the Lord visited Sarah as He had said and did for her as He had promised. ²Sarah was able to have a child and she gave birth to a son when Abraham was very old. He was born at the time the Lord said it would happen. ³Abraham gave the name Isaac to his son who was born to him by Sarah.

Kid-Builder Value

FAITH means believing the things that God has revealed about Himself and acting on those beliefs. Abraham believed God would give him a son because Abraham knew God would not break His promise.

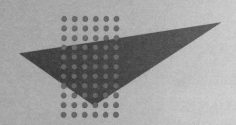

KID-BUILDER Questions

- The name *Isaac* means laughter. Why did they name their son Isaac?

- What circumstance in your life seems impossible to change? How can this story help you through times of doubt?

- What evidence do you see in your own life that God is faithful to keep His promises?

KID-BUILDER Prayer

Lord, help me to have faith, even when I have doubts about Your promises and Your ability to keep them.
In Jesus' name. Amen.

Memory Verse:
I am sure that God Who began the good work in you will keep on working in you until the day Jesus Christ comes again.   Phil. 1:6

GENESIS

Jacob and Esau

Genesis 25, 27, 28

Isaac grew up and married a woman named Rebekah. They, too, wanted children.

Isaac prayed to the Lord for his wife, because she could not give birth and the Lord answered him. Rebekah was able to give birth. . . .

²⁴When the day came for her to give birth, there were two babies to be born. ²⁵The first to come out was red and he had hair all over his body. They gave him the name of Esau. ²⁶Then the brother was born. His hand was holding onto Esau's heel. So he was given the name of Jacob. . . .

²⁷When the boys grew older, Esau became a good hunter, a man of the field. But Jacob was a man of peace, living in tents. ²⁸Isaac showed favor to Esau, because he liked to eat the meat of the animals Esau killed. But Rebekah showed favor to Jacob.

²⁹As Jacob was getting food ready one day, Esau came in from the field and was very hungry. ³⁰Esau said to Jacob, "Let me eat some of that red meat,

for I am very hungry.". . . ³¹But Jacob said, "First, sell me your right of being a first-born." ³²Esau said, "See, I am about to die. So what good is my birth-right to me?" ³³Jacob said, "First give me your promise." So Esau promised, and sold his birth-right to Jacob. ³⁴Then Jacob gave Esau bread and vegetables, and Esau ate and drank. . . .

²⁷:¹Isaac was now old, and had become blind. He

called to his older son Esau. . . . ²Isaac said, "See, I am old. I do not know when I will die. ³Take your bow and arrows, and go out to the field to get meat for me. ⁴Get some food ready for me that I love. Bring it to me to eat, so that before I die I will pray that good will come to you."

⁵But Rebekah was listening while Isaac spoke to his son Esau. So when Esau went to the field to hunt for meat to bring home, ⁶Rebekah said to her son Jacob, "I heard your father talking to your brother Esau. . . . ⁸So now, my son, listen to what I tell you to do. ⁹Go to the flock and bring me two fat young goats. I will cook them into good-tasting food, just what your father loves to eat. ¹⁰Then you will take it to your father for him to eat. So before he dies he will pray for good to come to you."

¹¹Jacob said, . . . "But my brother Esau has much hair. And my skin is smooth. ¹²If my father touches me, he will think of me as one trying to fool him. . . . " ¹³His mother said, ". . . Do what I say." . . . ¹⁴So . . . his mother made good-tasting food, just what his father loved to eat. ¹⁵Then Rebekah took the best clothes that belonged to her older son Esau . . . and she put them on her younger son Jacob. ¹⁶She put the skins of the young goats on his

Kid-Builder Fact
Gen. 25:32 The *birthright* was the blessing and double share of wealth a father gave to his oldest son.

hands and on the smooth part of his neck. 17And she gave her son Jacob the bread and the good-tasting food she had made.

18Then he went to his father and said, . . . 19"I am Esau, your first-born. . . . Sit up and eat the meat I brought, so that you will pray that good will come to me." . . .

21Then Isaac said to Jacob, "Come near so I can touch you, my son, to know for sure if you are my son Esau or not." 22So Jacob came near his father Isaac. Isaac touched him, and said, "The voice is Jacob's voice. But the hands are Esau's hands."

23. . . So Isaac prayed that good would come to him. . . .

30When Isaac had finished praying that good would come to Jacob . . . his brother Esau came in from hunting. 31Then Esau . . . said, "Sit up, my father, and eat the meat your son has made ready, so you will pray that good will come to me." . . . Isaac said to him, "Who are you?" He answered, "I am your son, your first-born, Esau." . . . 35But Isaac said, "Your brother came in and fooled me. He has taken away the good that was to come to you. . . . 37See, I have made him to rule over you. . . . What then can I do for you, my son?"

38Esau said to his father, ". . . Pray that good will come to me also, O my father.". . .Then . . . Isaac answered him: . . . 40"You will live by your sword. And you will serve your brother. But when you

break loose, you will throw his load off your back."

⁴¹Esau hated Jacob because of the good that would come to him because of his father's prayer. Esau said to himself, "The days when I will have sorrow for the loss of my father are soon. Then I will kill my brother Jacob." ⁴²But the words of her older son Esau were told to Rebekah. She called . . . Jacob, and said to him, "See, your brother Esau comforts himself by planning to kill you. ⁴³So now, my son, do what I tell you. Get ready and go at once to my brother Laban at Haran. ⁴⁴Stay with him for a few days, until your brother's anger goes away. ⁴⁵When your brother's anger against you is gone, . . . then I will send for you and have you return from there. . . ."

²⁸:¹⁰Jacob left Beersheba and went toward Haran.

Kid-Builder Value
HONESTY includes both truthfulness in your speech and consistency in your conduct. Jacob was not honest when he tricked Isaac into giving him the family blessing that belonged to Esau.

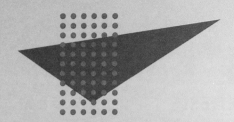

KID-BUILDER Questions

- How did Jacob trick Isaac? How did Esau react?

- Even though Esau had sold the birthright, Jacob was dishonest in the way he pretended to be Esau. Are there times when you are tempted to be dishonest? How do you feel when this happens?

- Why is it hard to be honest at times? How can God's Word help?

KID-BUILDER Prayer

Lord, when I'm tempted to lie in order to get my own way, give me strength to be honest.

In Jesus' name. Amen.

Memory Verse:
Make them holy for Yourself by the truth. Your Word is truth.

John 17:17

GENESIS

Joseph and His Brothers

Genesis 37—39, 42—46

The Lord changed Jacob's name to Israel and gave him twelve sons. Joseph was Jacob's favorite son.

Jacob lived in the land where his father had lived as a stranger, in the land of Canaan. ²This is the story of the children of Jacob and of their children.

When Joseph was seventeen years old, he was caring for the flock with his brothers. . . . ³Now Israel loved Joseph more than all his sons, because Joseph was born when he was an old man. And Israel made him a long coat of many colors. ⁴His brothers saw that their father loved him more than all his brothers. So they hated Joseph and could not speak a kind word to him.

⁵Then Joseph had a dream. . . . ⁶He said to [his brothers], "Listen to the dream that I have had. ⁷We were gathering grain in the field. My bundle of grain stood up. Your bundles of grain gathered around it and bowed down to my bundle." ⁸Then his brothers . . . hated him even more. . . .

¹²Then his brothers went to feed their father's flock in Shechem. ¹³Israel said to Joseph, ". . . Come, I will send you to them."
. . . Joseph followed his brothers and found them at Dothan.

¹⁸When they saw him far away, . . . they made plans to kill him. ¹⁹They said to one another, "Here comes this dreamer! ²⁰Now come and let us kill him and throw him into one of the deep holes. Then we will say that a wild animal ate him. And we will see what becomes of his dreams!"

²¹But Reuben [the oldest brother] heard this and saved him from their hands, saying, "Let us not kill him. ²². . . Throw him into this hole here in the place where no people live. But do not lay a hand on him." He wanted to be able to save Joseph

and return him to his father.

23So when Joseph came to his brothers, they tore off his coat. . . . 24And they took him and threw him into a hole. The hole was empty and had no water in it.

25Then they sat down to eat. When they looked up, they saw a group of Ishmaelites coming from Gilead. . . . 26Judah said to his brothers, "What do we get by killing our brother and covering his blood? 27Come, let us sell him to the Ishmaelites." . . . So [they] . . . sold him to the Ishmaelites for twenty pieces of silver. . . .

29. . .When [Reuben] saw that Joseph was not in the hole, he tore his clothes. 30He returned to his brothers and said, "The boy is not there! What can I do?" 31So they took Joseph's coat, killed a male goat, and put the blood on the coat. 32They sent the coat of many colors to their father. . . .

33Jacob looked at it and said, "It is my son's coat! A wild animal has eaten him! For sure Joseph has been torn to pieces!" 34So Jacob tore his clothes and . . . had sorrow for his son many days. 35All his sons and daughters tried to comfort him. But he would not be comforted. . . .

Kid-Builder Fact
Gen. 37:2 The twelve sons of Jacob were: Reuben, Simeon, Levi, Judah, Issachar, Zebulun, Joseph, Benjamin, Dan, Naphtali, Gad, and Asher.

36The Midianites [traders] sold Joseph in Egypt to Potiphar, the head of the soldiers of Pharaoh's house.

39:2The Lord was with Joseph, and all went well with him.

While in Potiphar's house, Joseph was falsely accused and thrown into prison. But God made everything go his way. After several years in prison, Joseph interpreted Pharaoh's dream and was put in charge of all of Egypt under Pharaoh.

42:6Joseph was the ruler of the land. He was the one who sold grain to all the people. . . . Joseph's brothers came and bowed to the ground in front of him. 7When Joseph saw his brothers, he knew who they were. But he acted like a stranger . . . to them. He said, "Where have you come from?" They answered, "From the land of Canaan, to buy food.

13. . . "Your servants are twelve brothers, the sons of one man in the land of Canaan. The youngest is now with our father. And one is no more." 14But Joseph said, . . . 15"By the life of Pharaoh, you will not leave this place unless your youngest brother comes here.". . .

17He put them . . . in prison for three days. 18Then Joseph said to them on the third day, 19". . . Let one of your brothers stay here in prison for all of you. But you others go and carry grain for your hungry families. 20Then bring your youngest brother to me. . . ." 21They said to one another, "For sure we

are guilty for what we did to our brother [Joseph].
. . . So this trouble has come to us."

22Reuben answered them, "Did I not tell you, 'Do not sin against the boy?' But you would not listen. Now we must pay for his blood." . . . 24Joseph went away from them and cried. Then he returned . . . and took Simeon from them and put chains on him. . . .

29When they came to their father Jacob in the land of Canaan, they told him all that had happened to them. . . .

43:2When they had eaten all the grain they had brought from Egypt, their father said to them, "Go again and buy us a little food." 3But Judah told him, . . ."If you send our brother with us, we will go to Egypt to buy you food. 5But if you do not send him, we will not go. . . . "

11Then . . . Israel said to them, ". . . 12Take twice as much money with you. . . . 13Take your brother also. . . . 14May the All-powerful God give you such favor with the man that he may let your other brother and Benjamin return. . . ."

15The men took . . . money, and Benjamin . . . to Egypt. . . . 16When Joseph saw Benjamin with them, he said to the man who took care of his house, "Bring the men into the house. . . . The men will eat with me at noon.". . .

26When Joseph came home . . . 27[he] asked them about their well-being. He said, "Is your father . . . still alive?" 28And they said, "Your servant, our father is well. He is still alive." . . .

29As he looked up, he saw his brother Benjamin, his mother's son. . . . 30Then Joseph went out in a hurry. For he had much feeling for his brother. He went in his room and cried. 31Then he washed his face and came out. . . .

44:1Then Joseph told the man who took care of his house, "Fill the men's bags with as much food as they can carry. And put each man's money in his bag. 2Put my silver cup in the bag of the youngest. . . . " And he did what Joseph had told him to do. 3Early in the morning the men were sent away. . . . 4When they had left the city and were not far away, Joseph said to the man who took care of his house, "Get up and follow the men. . . . [S]ay to them, '. . . Why have you stolen the silver cup? . . .' "

6So he . . . spoke these words to them. 7And they said, . . . 9"If the cup is found with any of your servants, let him be put to death. And the others of us will be your servants.". . .

11Then each man . . . opened [his bag]. . . . The cup was found in Benjamin's bag. 13. . . After each man loaded his donkey again, they returned to the city.

14When Judah and his brothers came to Joseph's house. . . . [t]hey fell to the ground in front of him. 15Joseph said to them, . . . "The person who was found with the cup will be my servant. But you others may go in peace to your father."

[18]Then Judah . . . said, "O my lord, . . . [33]let your servant stay and work for my lord, instead of the boy . . . For how can I return to my father if the boy is not with me? I am afraid to see the sorrow that my father would suffer."

[45:1]Then Joseph could [no longer] hide his feelings. . . . He cried, "Send all the people away from me." So no one was with him when Joseph told his brothers who he was. . . . [3]Joseph said to his brothers, "I am Joseph! Is my father still alive?" But his brothers could not answer him, for they were afraid. . . .

[4]Joseph said, . . . "I am your brother Joseph, whom you sold into Egypt. [5]But do not be troubled or angry with yourselves because you sold me here. For God sent me before you to save your life. . . . [8]So it was not you who sent me here, but God. . . . [9]Hurry and go to my father. Say to him, 'Your son Joseph says to you, "God has made me ruler of all Egypt. Come to me, and do not wait. [10]You will live in the land of Goshen, you and your children and grandchildren, your flocks and cattle, and all you have. . . . [11]There I will take care of you. . . .' "

Kid-Builder Value
FORGIVENESS refers to blotting out sin and guilt. Joseph forgave his brothers, even though they had wronged him.

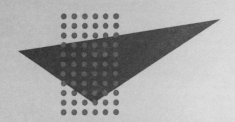

KID-BUILDER Questions

- Why did Joseph's brothers have to go to Egypt?

- When the brothers realized who Joseph was, they were troubled. Why? How did Joseph comfort them?

- Joseph's brothers were mean to Joseph. Joseph could have held a grudge, but he chose to forgive them instead. Have you ever been tempted to hold a grudge against someone? What happened?

- How do you feel trying to get even with someone? How do you think the other person feels?

KID-BUILDER Prayer

Lord, when I'm tempted to try to get even, help me remember to forgive instead, like Joseph.

In Jesus' name. Amen.

Memory Verse:
Love does not do the wrong thing. . . . Love does not remember the suffering that comes from being hurt by someone.   I Cor. 13:5

THE LAW

Exodus

Exodus is the second book written by Moses. It tells the story of the Hebrews and their journey from Egypt to the promised land of Canaan.

After Joseph died, God continued to bless the Hebrews and they grew in numbers. Egyptian rulers became afraid and thought they could control the growing population by making the Hebrews their slaves. God rescued His people and chose Moses to lead them away from Egypt.

Leviticus

While wandering in the wilderness on the way to the promised land, Moses wrote a third book called *Leviticus* (luh-VIT-eh-cuss). This book is called the priest's handbook, because it explains the rules for religious ceremonies, as well as for everyday life—what to eat and how to act. God again promises to be with His people, and He reminds them that keeping His commands is part of living for Him.

EXODUS

Miriam Helps Moses

Exodus 1—2

Hundreds of years passed after Joseph's death. The Israelites still lived in Egypt.

Joseph and all his brothers died and all their families of that time. ⁷But the sons of Israel had many children, and the people became many in number. There were so many that the land was filled with them.

⁸Then a new king came into power over Egypt. He did not know Joseph. ⁹He said to his people, "See, the people of Israel are too many and too powerful for us. ¹⁰Come, let us be wise in how we act towards them, or they will become more in number. If there is a war, they might join with those who hate us. They might fight against us and then leave the land."

¹¹So they put men in power over them to make them work hard. And they built the store-cities Pithom and Raamses for Pharaoh the king. ¹²But the more the Egyptians made them suffer, the more they became until they spread throughout

the land. So the Egyptians were afraid of the people of Israel. . . .

¹⁵Then the king of Egypt spoke to the Hebrew nurses. . . . ¹⁶He said, "When you are helping the Hebrew women to give birth, and see the baby before the mother does, if it is a son, kill him. But if it is a daughter, let her live." ¹⁷But the nurses feared God. They did not do what the king of Egypt told them. They let the boys live. . . . ²²Then Pharaoh told all his people, "Throw every son who is born to the Hebrews into the Nile. But keep every daughter alive."

²:¹Now a man of the house of Levi married a daughter of Levi. ²She . . . gave birth to a son. When she saw that he was beautiful, she hid him for three months. ³But the time came when she could hide him no longer. So she took a basket made from grass, and covered it with tar and put the child in it. And she set it in the grass by the side of the Nile. ⁴His sister stayed to watch and find out what would happen to him.

⁵Then the daughter of Pharaoh came to wash herself in the Nile. Her young women walked

Kid-Builder Fact
Exod. 2:3 Papyrus—a tall plant that grows in water and swampy places—was made into sheets for writing. Although our word *paper* comes from papyrus, papyrus was not like the paper we use today. It was also used to make light boats or canoes. The little basket in the Nile River was probably made of papyrus.

beside the Nile. She saw the basket in the tall grass and sent the woman who served her to get it. 6She opened it and saw the child. The boy was crying. She had pity on him and said, "This is one of the Hebrews' children." 7Then his sister said to Pharaoh's daughter, "Should I go and call a nurse for you from the Hebrew women, to nurse the child for you?" 8Pharaoh's daughter said to her, "Go." So the girl went and called the child's mother. 9Then Pharaoh's daughter said to her, "Take this child away and nurse him for me. And I will pay you." So the woman took the child and nursed him. 10The child grew, and she brought him to Pharaoh's daughter. And he became her son. She gave him the name Moses, saying, "Because I took him out of the water."

Kid-Builder Value

RESOURCEFULNESS is the ability to figure out ways to get a job done. Miriam and her mother showed resourcefulness when they hid Moses from Pharaoh.

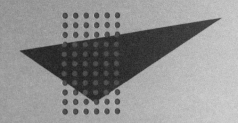

KID-BUILDER Questions

- Why did Pharaoh want to kill the Hebrew boys?

- What do you have that you can use to help others?

- How do people in your family show concern for each other?

KID-BUILDER Prayer

Lord, open my eyes to opportunities where I can help others.   In Jesus' name. Amen.

Memory Verse:
Do for other people what you would like to have them do for you.

Luke 6:31

EXODUS

Moses at the Burning Bush

Exodus 3—4

When Moses was forty years old, he killed an Egyptian who had beaten a Hebrew man. Because of this crime, Pharaoh wanted to kill Moses. But Moses ran away from Egypt and went to live for forty years in the land of Midian. There he married and became a shepherd.

Now Moses was taking care of the flock of his father-in-law Jethro, the religious leader of Midian. He led the flock to the west side of the desert, and came to Horeb, the mountain of God. ²There the Angel of the Lord showed Himself to Moses in a burning fire from inside a bush. Moses looked and saw that the bush was burning with fire, but it was not being burned up. ³So Moses said, "I must step aside and see this great thing, why the bush is not being burned up."

⁴The Lord . . . called to him from inside the bush, saying, "Moses, Moses!" Moses answered, "Here I am." ⁵God said, "Do not come near. Take your shoes off your feet. For the place where you are

standing is holy ground." 6He said also, "I am the God of Abraham, the God of Isaac, and the God of Jacob." Then Moses hid his face. For he was afraid to look at God.

7The Lord said, "I have seen the suffering of My people in Egypt. . . . 8So I have come down to

save them from the power of the Egyptians. . . . 10Now come, and I will send you to Pharaoh. . . ."

11But Moses said to God, "Who am I to go to Pharaoh and bring the people of Israel out of Egypt?" 12God said, "But I will be with you. And this will be something special for you to see to know that I have sent you: When you have brought the people out of Egypt, you will worship God at this mountain."

13Then Moses said to God, "See, I am going to the people of Israel, and I will say to them, 'The God of your fathers has sent me to you.' Now they might say to me, 'What is His name?' What should I say to them?" 14And God said to Moses, "I AM

WHO I AM." And He said, "Say to the Israelites, 'I AM has sent me to you.'... I have visited you and have seen what has been done to you in Egypt. [17]I promise to bring you out of the suffering of Egypt to... a land flowing with milk and honey."...

[4:1]Then Moses answered, "What if they will not believe me or listen to me? ..." [2]The Lord said to him, "What is that in your hand?" Moses said, "A stick." [3]Then the Lord said, "Throw it on the ground." So Moses threw it on the ground, and it became a snake. And Moses ran from it. [4]But the Lord said to Moses, "Put out your hand and take it by its tail." So Moses put out his hand and caught it. And it became a stick in his hand. [5]The Lord said, "By seeing this they may believe that the Lord, the God of their fathers . . . has shown Himself to you."

[6]The Lord said to him, "Put your hand inside your coat." So Moses put his hand inside his coat. When he took it out, his hand had a bad skin disease and was white as snow. [7]Then God said, "Put your hand inside your coat again." So Moses put his hand inside his coat again. When he took it out of his coat, he saw that it had become like his other

Kid-Builder Value
HOLINESS refers to something or someone that is set apart as being sacred, consecrated, or dedicated. Moses faced the holiness of God at the burning bush.

flesh. [8]God said, "If they will not listen to you or believe you when they are shown the first thing, they may believe when this is shown to them. . . ."

[10]Moses said to the Lord, "Lord, I am not a man of words. I have never been. . . . I am slow in talking and it is difficult for me to speak." [11]Then the Lord said to him, "Who has made man's mouth? Who makes a man not able to speak or hear? . . . Is it not I, the Lord? [12]So go now. And I will be with your mouth. I will teach you what to say."

[13]But Moses said, "O Lord, I ask of You, send some other person."

[14]Then the anger of the Lord burned against Moses. He said, "Is not Aaron the Levite your brother? I know he can speak well. Also, he is coming to meet you. . . . I will be with your mouth and his mouth. I will teach you what you are to do. [16] He will speak to the people for you. . . . [17]You will take this special stick in your hand. And you will use it to make the special things happen for the people to see."

[18]Then Moses left and returned to Jethro his father-in-law. . . . [19]The Lord said to Moses in Midian, "Return to Egypt. For all the men who wanted to kill you are dead." [20]So Moses took his wife and sons and . . . returned to the land of Egypt. Moses also took the special stick of God in his hand.

KID-BUILDER Questions

- What unusual sight did Moses see near Mount Horeb?

- Why did Moses have to take off his shoes?

- God is holy and deserves to be respected. How can you show respect for His holiness in your worship?

KID-BUILDER Prayer

Lord, You are holy and I worship You.
                                    In Jesus' name. Amen.

Memory Verse:
The Lord is right and good in all His ways, and kind in all His works.
                                                    Ps. 145:17

EXODUS

Red Sea Escape

Exodus 13—15

Because Pharaoh kept refusing to let the Israelites leave, God sent ten plagues on the land. The last plague caused the deaths of all the Egyptian first-born—those of people and of animals. After that, the Israelites were allowed to leave Egypt.

So God led the people through the place where no people live to get to the Red Sea. . . . 21The Lord went before them, in a pillar of cloud during the day to lead them on the way, and in a pillar of fire during the night to give them light. So they could travel day and night. 22The pillar of cloud during the day and the pillar of fire during the night did not leave the people. . . .

14:5When the king of Egypt was told that the people had left, Pharaoh and his servants changed their minds about the people. . . . 6So he made his [chariot] ready and took his people with him. 7He took 600 of the best [chariots], and all the other [chariots] of Egypt in the care of leaders. 8The Lord made the heart of Pharaoh, king of Egypt

hard. And Pharaoh went to catch the people of Israel, who were leaving without fear. . . .

10When Pharaoh came near, the people of Israel looked and saw the Egyptians coming after them. And they were filled with fear and cried out to the Lord. 11Then they said to Moses, "Is it because there were no graves in Egypt that you have taken us away to die in the place where no people live? What have you done to us, in bringing us out of Egypt? 12Did we not tell you in Egypt, 'Leave us alone and let us serve the Egyptians'? It would have been better for us to serve the Egyptians than to die here." 13But Moses said to the people, "Do not be afraid! Be strong, and see how the Lord will save you today. For the Egyptians you have seen today, you will never see again. 14The Lord will fight for you. All you have to do is keep still."

15Then the Lord said to Moses, "Why do you cry to me? Tell the people of Israel to keep going. 16Lift up your special stick and put out your hand over the sea, and divide it. Then the people of Israel will go through the sea on dry land. 17I will make the Egyptians' hearts hard, so they will go after them.

Kid-Builder Fact
Exod. 13:18 The Red Sea is a large body of water near Egypt. It is 1,300 miles long stretching from the Indian Ocean to the Suez Canal. Although the Red Sea is salty, its waters are green and clear. Many fish and other forms of life thrive there.

And I will be honored through Pharaoh and his whole army, his [chariots], and his horsemen. . . ."

21Then Moses put out his hand over the sea. And the Lord moved the sea all night by a strong east wind. So the waters were divided. 22And the people of Israel went through the sea on dry land. The waters were like a wall to them on their right and on their left. 23Then the Egyptians followed them. All Pharaoh's horses and [chariots] and horsemen went in the sea after them. 24In the morning hours, the Lord looked down on the Egyptian army through the fire and cloud. And He made the Egyptian army afraid. 25He made the wheels of their [chariots] come off, so it was hard for the [chariots] to be moved. So the Egyptians said, "Let us run away from Israel. For the Lord is fighting for them against the Egyptians."

26Then the Lord said to Moses, "Put out your hand over the sea. And the waters will flow over the Egyptians, and over their [chariots] and their horsemen." 27And when the morning came, the Egyptians ran into the wall of water as the sea returned to the way it was before. The Lord destroyed the Egyptians in the sea. 28The waters returned and covered the [chariots] and the horsemen and Pharaoh's whole army that had gone in the sea after them. Not even one of them was left. . . .

30So the Lord saved Israel that day from the

Egyptians. And Israel saw the Egyptians dead beside the sea. 31Israel saw the great power which the Lord had used against the Egyptians. And the people had fear of the Lord. They believed in the Lord and in His servant Moses.

15:1Then Moses and the people of Israel sang this song to the Lord, saying, "I will sing to the Lord, for He is praised for His greatness. He has thrown the horse and horseman into the sea. 2The Lord is my strength and song. He is the One Who saves me. . . . He is my father's God and I will honor Him."

Kid-Builder Value
PRAISE includes words or actions that give honor to someone. Moses and the people had reason to praise God after He rescued them from the Egyptians at the Red Sea.

KID-BUILDER Questions

- How did God lead the Israelites by day? By night?

- The Israelites were excited to leave Egypt. But what happened when they got to the Red Sea?

- How did God rescue them?

- When someone does something great for you, how do you respond?

- God does great things today! How has He helped you? How can you give Him praise?

KID-BUILDER Prayer

Lord, thank You, for the many times You have helped me! You have helped me in so many ways! Thank You!   *In Jesus' name. Amen.*

Memory Verse:
Praise the Lord! Praise God in His holy place! Praise Him in the heavens of His power!   Ps. 150:1

EXODUS

The Ten Commandments

Exodus 19—20

In the third month after the people of Israel left Egypt, they came to the Sinai desert on the same day. ²They had left Rephidim and had come to the Sinai desert. There Israel set up their tents in front of the mountain. . . .

⁹The Lord said to Moses, "See, I will come to you in a thick cloud. So the people may hear when I speak with you, and may believe you forever. . . . Go to the people. Today and tomorrow set them apart to be holy. Have them wash their clothes. ¹¹And let them be ready for the third day. For on the third day people will see the Lord come down on Mount Sinai. ¹²Let the people know the places all around that they must not pass. Tell them, 'Be careful that you do not go up on the mountain or touch any place around it. Whoever touches the mountain will be put to death.' ¹³. . . When a long sound from a horn is heard, they may come up to the mountain." . . .

²⁰:¹Then God spoke all these words, saying, ²"I

am the Lord your God, Who brought you out of the land of Egypt, out of the house where you were servants.

[3]"Have no gods other than Me.

[4]"Do not make for yourselves a god to look like anything that is in heaven above or on the earth below or in the waters under the earth.

[5]"Do not worship them or work for them. For I, the Lord your God, am a jealous God. I punish the children, even the great-grandchildren, for the sins of their fathers who hate Me. [6]But I show loving-kindness to thousands of those who love Me and keep My Laws.

[7]"Do not use the name of the Lord your God in a false way. For the Lord will punish the one who uses His name in a false way.

[8]"Remember the Day of Rest, to keep it holy. [9]Six days you will do all your work. [10]But the seventh day is a Day of Rest to the Lord your God. You . . . must not do any work on this day. [11]For in six days the Lord made the heavens, the earth, the sea and all that is in them. And He rested on the seventh day. So the Lord gave honor to the Day of Rest and made it holy.

Kid-Builder Value

SELF-DISCIPLINE is the willingness to correct yourself in order to make yourself a better person. Discipline does not mean punishment. It means that God has given us guidelines so that we can become more spiritually healthy.

¹²"Honor your father and your mother, so your life may be long in the land the Lord your God gives you.

¹³"Do not kill other people.

¹⁴"Do not do sex sins.

¹⁵"Do not steal

¹⁶"Do not tell a lie about your neighbor

¹⁷"Do not have a desire for your neighbor's house. Do not have a desire for his wife or his male servant, his female servants, or his bull or his donkey or anything that belongs to your neighbor."

¹⁸All the people heard and saw the thunder and lightning, the sound of the horn, and the mountain smoking. And when the people saw it, they shook with fear and stood far away.

KID-BUILDER Questions

- What did God tell the Israelites about worshiping Him? Why is that important?

- The Ten Commandments were given so that we would have guidelines to keep us from sin. But God knew that we couldn't keep them without His help. What are some rules you need help to keep?

- Having self-discipline means that we try to keep the rules. We discipline ourselves by practicing right behavior. What are some rules your family has? Why is it important to obey them?

KID-BUILDER Prayer

Lord, I need You! I can't live a life that will please You without Your help.   In Jesus' name. Amen.

Memory Verse:
A young man makes himself known by his actions and proves if his ways are pure and right.

Prov. 20:11

THE LAW

Numbers

Numbers is the fourth book written by Moses. In the Hebrew Bible, this book is called *In the Wilderness,* which describes what it is about. It tells of the ups and downs of the Israelites from their slavery in Egypt until they entered the promised land. *Numbers* shows how God took care of His people even when they disobeyed Him. It shows how patient He is and how much He cares about all the details of His people's lives. It also shows that God does punish sin.

Deuteronomy

Deuteronomy (DOO-ter-ON-uh-mee) is the fifth book in the Bible. It begins with the Israelites camped by the Jordan River after forty years of wandering in the wilderness. They were ready to enter the promised land. Many instructions for living are given in this book.

NUMBERS

Twelve Spies Are Sent to Canaan

Numbers 13—14

Finally the people have arrived at the edge of the promised land of Canaan.

The Lord said to Moses, 2"Send men to look over the land of Canaan which I am going to give the people of Israel. Send a man from each of their fathers' families. . . ." 3So Moses sent them from the desert of Paran, as the Lord had told him. All of the men were heads of the people of Israel. 4[Among these were] . . . 6Caleb the son of Jephunneh . . . 8 [and] Hoshea the son of Nun. . . . 16Moses called Hoshea the son of Nun, Joshua.

17Moses sent them to look over the land of Canaan. He said to them, "Go up there into the Negev. Then go up into the hill country. 18See what the land is like. See if the people who live in it are strong or weak, and if they are few or many. . . . 20Find out . . . if there are trees in it or not. Then try to get some of the fruit of the land.". . .

21So they went up and looked over the land. . . .

23Then they came to the valley of Eschol. They

cut down a branch from there with some grapes on it. And they carried it on a long piece of wood between two men, with some pomegranates and figs. . . .

25They returned from looking over the land after forty days. 26And they came to Moses and Aaron and to all the people of Israel. . . . 27They told Moses, "We went to the land where you sent us. It does flow with milk and honey. This is its fruit. 28But the people who live in the land are strong. The cities have walls and are very large. . . ."

30Then Caleb told the people in front of Moses to be quiet. And he said, "Let us go up at once and take the land. For we are well able to take it in battle." 31But the men who had gone up with him said, "We are not able to go against the people. They are too strong for us. . . ."

14:2All the people of Israel complained against Moses and Aaron, and said to them, "If only we had died in the land of Egypt! . . . 3Why is the Lord bringing us into this land to be killed by the sword? . . . 4Let us choose a leader and return to Egypt."

5Then Moses and Aaron fell on their faces in front of all . . . the people of Israel. 6And Joshua . . . and Caleb . . . tore their clothes. . . . 7They said to all the people of Israel, "The land we passed through to look over is a very good land. 8If the Lord is pleased with us, then He will bring us into

this land and give it to us. . . . 9Only do not go against the Lord. And do not be afraid of the people of the land. . . ." 10But all the people said to throw stones at Joshua and Caleb. Then the shining greatness of the Lord was seen in the meeting tent by all the people of Israel.

11The Lord said to Moses, "How long will this people turn away from Me? How long will they not believe in Me, even after all the great works I have done among them? 12I will punish them with disease, and will not give them the land. And I will make you into a nation greater and stronger than they."

13But Moses said to the Lord, . . . 19"I pray that You will forgive the sin of this people by the greatness of Your loving-kindness. . . ."

20So the Lord said, "I have forgiven them as you asked. . . . 27How long will this sinful people speak against Me? I have heard the people of Israel complaining against Me. 28Say to them, 'As I live. . . 29[y]our dead bodies will fall in this desert, all of you who were numbered from twenty years old and older, who have spoken against Me. 30For sure, not one will go into the land where I have promised to have you live, except Caleb . . . and Joshua the son of Nun. . . . 34You looked over the land for forty days. For each day you will carry your guilt a year, forty years. And you will know that I am against you. . . ."

39When Moses told these words to all the people of Israel, the people were filled with much sorrow.

Kid-Builder Value
TRUSTWORTHINESS means that you are dependable and that other people can count on you. Because they had proven themselves in the past and trusted God, Joshua and Caleb's report to the people was trustworthy.

KID-BUILDER Questions

- What did most of the spies say about the land? What did Joshua and Caleb say?

- Who did the people believe? What happened as a result?

- Have you ever trusted someone who turned out to be untrustworthy? What happened?

- How trustworthy would your friends say you are?

KID-BUILDER Prayer

Dear Lord, help me do the things that inspire trust in others.   *In Jesus' name. Amen.*

Memory Verse:
How happy is the man who has made the Lord his trust, and has not turned to the proud or to the followers of lies.   Psalm 40:4

DEUTERONOMY

Joshua Becomes the New Leader

Deuteronomy 31, 34

Then Moses spoke these words to all Israel, . . . "I am 120 years old today. I am no longer able to come and go. And the Lord has told me, 'You will not cross this Jordan.' ³The Lord your God Himself will cross before you. He will destroy these nations in front of you. And you will take their place. Joshua will cross before you also, as the Lord has said. . . . ⁶Be strong and have strength of heart. Do not be afraid or shake with fear. . . . For the Lord your God is the One Who goes with you. . . . He will not leave you alone."

⁷Then Moses called Joshua and said to him in front of all Israel, "Be strong and have strength of heart. For you will go with this people into the land the Lord has promised to their fathers to give them. And you will bring them in to take it. ⁸The Lord . . . will be with you . . . and will not leave you alone. Do not be afraid or troubled."

³⁴:¹Now Moses went up from the valleys of Moab to Mount Nebo, to the top of Pisgah, beside

Jericho. And the Lord showed him all the land. . . . [4]Then the Lord said to him, "This is the land I promised Abraham, Isaac and Jacob, saying, 'I will give it to your children.' I have let you see it with your eyes, but you will not go there." [5]So Moses the servant of the Lord died there in the land of Moab, as the Word of the Lord said. [6]And He buried him . . . in the land of Moab, beside Beth-peor. But no man knows where he is buried to this day. [7]Moses was 120 years old when he died. But his eyes were not weak, and his strength had not left him. [8]The children of Israel cried for Moses . . . for thirty days. Then the days of crying and sorrow for Moses came to an end.

[9]Now Joshua the son of Nun was filled with the spirit of wisdom, for Moses had laid his hands on him. So the people of Israel listened to him and did what the Lord had told Moses. [10]There never has been another man who speaks for God in Israel like Moses. The Lord knew him face to face. [11]There has never been another like him who has done all the powerful works the Lord sent him to do in the land of Egypt.

Kid-Builder Value
RESPONSIBILITY means you are able and willing to do what you say you'll do. In the wilderness, Joshua proved that he was a responsible person, so God chose him to be the new leader of the Israelites.

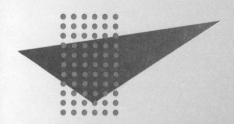

KID-BUILDER Questions

- What was Joshua picked to do?

- Joshua had a big responsibility. What was the biggest responsibility you ever had?

- Being a leader can be scary, especially if there is no one to help you. Who can you count on to help out when you have a big job?

KID-BUILDER Prayer

Lord, I need Your help to face my responsibilities.
In Jesus' name. Amen.

Memory Verse:
The Lord is the One Who goes before you. He will be with you. He will be faithful to you and will not leave you alone. Do not be afraid or troubled.   Deuteronomy 31:8

HISTORY

The Old Testament Books of History

The next twelve books in the Bible are known as the books of *Old Testament History*. These books include Joshua, Judges, Ruth, I and II Samuel, I and II Kings, I and II Chronicles, Ezra, Nehemiah, and Esther. They tell the history of the Jewish people from the time of their settling in the promised land to captivity in a strange land.

Joshua

The Book of *Joshua*, which Joshua wrote, is the first of the history books. It tells about the campaigns of the Israelites in conquering Canaan and explains how the land was divided among the various tribes. The following two stories—"The Walls of Jericho Fall" and "Achan's Sin"— are two examples of the kind of stories you will find in this book. *Joshua* is a book about obedience and making decisions. The lessons the Israelites learned during this time are useful in helping us make right choices today.

JOSHUA

The Walls of Jericho Fall

Joshua 6

The people of Israel have crossed over the Jordan River with God's help. Now they are ready to do battle to take the land.

Now the gates of Jericho were all shut because of the people of Israel. No one went out and no one came in. ²The Lord said to Joshua, "See, I have given Jericho into your hand, with its king and soldiers. ³Walk around the city. Have all the men of war go around the city once. Do this for six days. ⁴Seven religious leaders will carry seven rams' horns. They will walk in front of the special box of the agreement. Then on the seventh day you will walk around the city seven times. And the religious leaders will blow horns. ⁵When you hear the long sound of the ram's horn, all the people should call out with a loud noise. The wall of the city will fall to the ground. . . ."

⁸When Joshua had spoken to the people, the seven religious leaders carrying the seven rams' horns before the Lord walked on and blew the

horns. And the special box of the agreement of the Lord followed them. 9The men ready for battle went in front of the religious leaders who blew the horns. The other soldiers came behind the special box of the agreement while the horns sounded without stopping. 10But Joshua told the people, "Do not call out or let your voice be heard. Not a word should come from your mouth until the day I tell you to call out. Then you must call out." 11So he had the special box of the agreement taken around the city once. Then they returned to the tents and stayed there through the night. . . .

14 . . . They did this for six days.

15On the seventh day they got up early at the rising of the sun. They walked around the city . . . seven times. 16The seventh time, when the religious leaders blew their horns, Joshua said to the people, "Call out! For the Lord has given you the city! 17The city and all that is in it must be destroyed because everything in it belongs to the Lord. Only Rahab . . . and all who are with her in the house will live, because she hid the men we sent. 18But keep yourselves from the things that are to be destroyed. Or while you give them up to

Kid-Builder Fact
Josh. 6:1 Walls in Bible times were the major way of defending cities against attack. Every ancient city had huge walls made of mud, stones, or brick. Some of these walls are still standing today.

be destroyed, you might desire them. Then you would make the camp of Israel sinful also, and bring trouble on it. [19]But all the silver and gold and objects of brass and iron are holy to the Lord. They will go into the store-house of the Lord." [20]So the people called out and the religious leaders blew the horns. When the people heard the sound of the horns, they called out even louder. And the wall fell to the ground. All the people went straight in and took the city. [21]They destroyed everything in the city, both man and woman, young and old, cattle, sheep, and donkey, with the sword. . . .

[24]Then they burned the city with fire, and all that was in it. Only the silver and gold and objects of brass and iron they put into the store-house of the holy tent of the Lord. [25]Joshua saved the life of Rahab . . . and those of her father's house and all she had. She has lived among Israel to this day, because she hid the men Joshua had sent to look over Jericho. . . .

[27]So the Lord was with Joshua. He was well known and respected in all the land.

Kid-Builder Value
OBEDIENCE is doing what you're instructed to do.
Obedience to the Lord led to victory at Jericho.

KID-BUILDER Questions

- What instructions did the Israelites follow?
- What happened to the walls of Jericho?
- Disobedience would have meant disaster for the Israelites. They followed God's instructions exactly. What instructions do you have to follow daily?

KID-BUILDER Prayer

Lord, help me obey Your Word and walk in Your ways.   *In Jesus' name. Amen.*

Memory Verse:
You must love the Lord your God with all your heart and with all your soul and with all your mind.   Matt. 22:37b

JOSHUA

Achan's Sin

Joshua 7

The people of Israel sinned with the things that were to be destroyed [in the city of Jericho]. Achan, the son of Carmi, . . . from the family of Judah, took some of the things that were to be destroyed. So the Lord was very angry with the people of Israel.

²Joshua sent men from Jericho to Ai. . . . He said to them, "Go and look over the land in secret." So the men went and looked over Ai. ³When they returned to Joshua, they said, ". . . Only about 2000 or 3000 men need to go to Ai. Do not make the whole army fight, for the people of Ai are few." ⁴ So about 3000 men of Israel went, but they ran away from the men of Ai. ⁵The men of Ai killed about thirty-six of their men and . . . more on the way down. So the hearts of the people became weak. . . .

⁶Then Joshua and the leaders of Israel tore their clothes. They fell with their faces on the ground in front of the special box of the agreement until evening. . . . ⁷Joshua said, "O Lord God, why did

You ever bring this nation over the Jordan, only to give us into the hand of the Amorites to be destroyed? . . ."

¹⁰The Lord said to Joshua, "Get up! Why have you fallen on your face? ¹¹Israel has sinned. . . . They have even taken some of the things that were to be destroyed. . . . I will not be with you any more unless you destroy the things among you that should be destroyed.¹³". . . Set apart the people. . . . ¹⁴In the morning you must come near by your family groups. . . . The family which the Lord takes must come near by tents. And the tent which the Lord takes must come near man by man. ¹⁵Then the one who is taken with the things which should have been destroyed must be burned with fire, he and all that belongs to him. . . .' "

16So Joshua got up early in the morning and brought Israel near by family groups. The family group of Judah was taken. 17He brought the family group of Judah near. And he took the family of the Zerahites. He brought the family of the Zerahites near man by man. Zabdi was taken. 18Then he brought those of Zabdi's tent near man by man. And Achan, son of Carmi, son of Zabdi . . . was taken. 19Joshua said to Achan, "My son . . . Tell me now what you have done. Do not hide it from me." 20Achan answered Joshua, saying, "It is true. I have sinned against the Lord, the God of Israel. . . . 21I saw among what was left of the city a beautiful coat from Shinar. I saw 200 pieces of silver, and a large piece of gold as heavy as fifty pieces of silver. . . . They are hidden in the ground inside my tent. . . . with the silver under it."

22So Joshua sent men to the tent. There they found it, with the silver under it. 23They took these things from inside the tent and brought them to Joshua and all the people of Israel. And they laid

Kid-Builder Fact
Num. 14:44 The *special box* is the ark of the covenant. The ark of the covenant was a wooden chest covered with gold about 4 feet long, 2-1/2 feet wide, and 2-1/2 feet high. God told Moses how it should be built. It was carried on poles pushed through four golden rings on the corners. On top were two golden cherubim. The Ten Commandments written on stone tablets, a pot of manna, and the rod that Aaron used were inside this special box.

them down before the Lord. ²⁴Then Joshua and all Israel took Achan, . . . the silver, the coat, the large piece of gold, his sons and daughters, . . . and all that belonged to him. They brought them to the valley of Achor. ²⁵And Joshua said, "Why have you brought this trouble upon us? The Lord will trouble you this day." Then all Israel threw stones at them. After that they burned them with fire. ²⁶They put many stones over him. . . . Then the Lord was no longer angry. The name of that place has been called the Valley of Achor to this day.

Kid-Builder Value
COURAGE is the ability and willingness to stand firm when confronted by danger, fear, or peer pressure. Achan could have used more courage, rather than curiosity. His sin led to trouble for Israel.

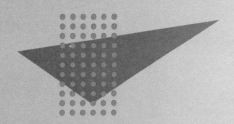

KID-BUILDER Questions

- Why were the Israelites defeated at Ai?

- Read Joshua 6:18 on page 79. What were God's instructions? What was Achan's sin?

- Disobedience meant death. Achan finally discovered courage when it came time to confess. When the going gets tough, how much courage do you have when it comes to standing up to a bully? admitting that you did wrong?

KID-BUILDER Prayer

I want to be strong and courageous. Thank You for always being with me.   In Jesus' name. Amen.

Kid-Builder Verse:

Have I not told you? Be strong and have strength of heart. Do not be afraid or lose faith. For the Lord your God is with you anywhere you go.   Josh. 1:9

Judges

Judges tells what happened to the Israelites during the 350 years before Saul became king. The book describes how the Israelites worshiped idols and other false gods like those of the neighboring countries. Because of the trouble neighboring people caused Israel, the Lord raised up leaders called judges. These leaders helped Israel fight against their enemies. *Judges* contains stories of Gideon, Samson, and other judges. The Israelites' experiences with their enemies are good reminders for us of the importance of following God.

Ruth

Ruth tells the story of a romance between a widow and one of her husband's relatives in the time of the judges. During a time when Israel's loyalty to God was up and down, Ruth chose to listen to God even when others refused to obey Him. It's not always easy to live for God when your friends do not, but the Book of *Ruth* tells you that God will do special things for you when you take a stand for Him.

Gideon Is Chosen

Judges 6—8

The people of Israel sinned in the eyes of the Lord. And the Lord gave them into the hands of Midian for seven years. . . . ⁴[The Midianites] would leave no food for Israel, and no sheep, cattle or donkeys ⁵. . . .They were like locusts, there were so many of them. . . . ⁶So Israel became very poor because of Midian. The people of Israel cried to the Lord. . . . ¹¹Then the angel of the Lord . . . ¹²showed himself to Gideon and said to him, "The Lord is with you, O powerful soldier." ¹³Gideon said to him, "O sir, if the Lord is with us, why has all this happened to us? . . ." ¹⁴The Lord looked at him and said, "Go in this strength of yours. And save Israel from the power of Midian. Have I not sent you?" ¹⁵Gideon said to Him, "O Lord, how can I save Israel? See, my family is the least in Manasseh. And I am the youngest in my father's house." ¹⁶But the Lord said to him, "For sure I will be with you. You will destroy Midian. . . ."

⁷:¹Then [Gideon] and all the people who were

with him got up early and set up their tents. . . .

²The Lord said to Gideon, "The people with you are too many for Me to give Midian into their hands. Israel might say with pride, 'Our own power has saved us.' ³So say to all the people, 'Whoever is afraid . . . may . . . return home.' " So 22,000 people returned. But 10,000 stayed.

⁴Then the Lord said to Gideon, "There are still too many people. Bring them down to the water. I will test them for you there. Whoever I say is to go with you will go. . . ." ⁵So Gideon brought the people down to the water. The Lord said, . . . "Divide every man who drinks the water as dogs drink with their tongues from every man who gets down on his knees to drink." ⁶There were 300 men who drank from their hand, putting their hand to their mouth. But all the rest of the people got down on their knees to drink water. ⁷The Lord said to Gideon, "I will save you with the 300 men who drank from their hands. . . ." ⁸Gideon sent all the other men of Israel to their tents. . . .

⁹That same night the Lord said to Gideon, ¹⁰". . . If you are afraid to [fight against Midian], go with your servant Purah down to their tents. ¹¹You will hear what they say. Then your hands will become strong enough to go down and fight against them." So he went with his servant Purah down to the side of the tents where [Midianite] soldiers were keeping watch. . . . ¹³When Gideon came, a man

was telling a dream to his friend. The man said, "I had a dream. A loaf of barley bread was rolling toward the tents of Midian. It came to the tent and hit it so it fell down. It turned it up-side-down so the tent fell apart." 14His friend answered and said, "This is nothing else but the sword of Gideon. . . . God has given Midian and all the army into his hand."

15 . . . [Gideon] bowed down and worshiped God.

Then he returned to the tents of Israel and said, "Get up! For the Lord has given the army of Midian into your hands." 16He divided the 300 men into three groups. He gave horns and empty pots with fire sticks inside to each of them. 17And he said to them, "Watch me, and do what I do. When I come to the side of their tents, do as I do. 18I and all those with me will blow the horns. Then you blow the horns all around the tents, and say, 'For the Lord and for Gideon!' "

19So Gideon and the 100 men who were with him came to the side of the tents. It was late in the night. Different soldiers had just come to keep watch. Then the men blew the horns and broke the pots that were in their hands. 20All three groups blew their horns and broke their pots. . . . And they called out, "A sword for the Lord and for Gideon!" 21. . . All the Midianite army . . . cried out and ran away. 22When the 300 horns were blown, the Lord made every man fight the man next to him among the tents. And the army ran away. . . .

8:28Midian was put under the power of the people of Israel. They did not lift up their heads any more. And the land had peace for forty years, during the life of Gideon.

Kid-Builder Value
CONFIDENCE is a feeling of security based on faith and trust. Gideon had confidence that the Lord would help the Israelites defeat the Midianites.

KID-BUILDER Questions

- What did the Lord want Gideon to do?

- How many men did Gideon start out with? How many men did Gideon take into battle against the Midianites?

- The defeat of the Midianites left no doubt that God had won the battle. What are some situations you have faced where you had no doubt that God helped you?

- When you think about the times God has helped you, how can that build confidence in Him?

KID-BUILDER Prayer

Lord, sometimes I depend on my feelings or another person instead of having confidence in You. I need Your strength every day. I'm glad I can count on You.

In Jesus' name. Amen.

Memory Verse:
My soul is quiet and waits for God alone. My hope comes from Him
Ps. 62:5

Ruth Is Loyal

Ruth 1—4

In the days when judges ruled, there was a time of no food in the land. A certain man of Bethlehem in Judah went to visit the land of Moab with his wife and his two sons. ²The name of the man was Elimelech. His wife's name was Naomi, and . . . his two sons were Mahlon and Chilion. . . . ³Elimelech died, and [Naomi] was left with her two sons, ⁴who had married Moabite women. The name of one was Orpah. The name of the other was Ruth. After living there about ten years, ⁵both Mahlon and Chilion died. . . .

⁶Then Naomi got ready to return from the land of Moab with her daughters-in-law. She had heard . . . that the Lord had brought food to His people. . . . Naomi said, "Return to your people, my daughters. Why should you go with me? Do I have more sons within me, who could become your husbands? . . ." Orpah kissed her mother-in-law [and said good-bye], but Ruth held on to her.

¹⁵Naomi said, "See, your sister-in-law has

returned to her people and her gods. Return after your sister-in-law." 16But Ruth said, "Do not beg me to leave you or turn away from following you. I will go where you go. . . . Your people will be my people, and your God will be my God. . . ."

19So they both went until they came to Bethlehem. The whole town of Bethlehem was happy because of them. . . .

2:1There was a man in the family of Naomi's husband . . . whose name was Boaz. He was a very rich man. . . . 2Ruth . . . said to Naomi, "Let me go to the field to gather grain behind someone who might show favor to me." Naomi said to her, "Go, my daughter." 3So Ruth went and gathered in the field behind those who picked the grain. She happened to come to the part of the field that belonged to Boaz. . . . 5Then Boaz said to his servant who was watching over those who gathered grain, "Whose young woman is this?" 6The servant . . . said, "She is the young Moabite woman who returned with Naomi from the land of Moab. . . ."

8Then Boaz said to Ruth, "Be careful to listen, my daughter. Do not go to gather grain in another field. Do not leave this one, but stay here with my

Kid-Builder Fact
Ruth 2:15 In the Old Testament law, farmers were told they should let the poor come into their fields and pick up grain that was left in the field.

women who gather grain...." [10]Then she got down with her face to the ground and said to him, "Why have I found favor in your eyes? Why do you care about me? I am a stranger from another land." [11]Boaz said ... "I have heard about all you have done for your mother-in-law after the death of your husband.... [12]May the Lord pay you for your work."...

[17]So Ruth gathered grain in the field until evening. Then she beat out what she had gathered. It was enough barley to fill a basket. [18]She picked it up and went into the city to show her mother-in-law what she had gathered.... [19]Her mother-in-law said..., "Where did you gather grain today? ... May good come to the man who showed you favor." So Ruth told her mother-in-law, "The name of the man ... is Boaz." [20]Naomi said, "... The man is ... of our family."...

[3:1]Naomi said to [Ruth], "My daughter, should I not look for a home for you? ... Go down to the grain-floor. But do not let the man know who you are until he has finished eating and drinking. [4]When [Boaz] lies down, watch where he lies. Go in and take the covers off his feet and lie down. Then he will tell you what to do."...

Ruth did everything her mother-in-law told her to do. According to custom, uncovering Boaz's feet meant that Ruth wanted to be his wife. Boaz agreed to marry Ruth, if the nearer kinsman would not marry her.

4:1Boaz went up to the gate and sat down there. He saw the in-law of the family that he had spoken about pass by. So Boaz said, "Come here, friend, and sit down." So the man came and sat down. . . . ³Then Boaz said to the close in-law, "Naomi has returned from the land of Moab. She is selling the piece of land which belonged to our brother Elimelech. . . . ⁵The day you buy the field from Naomi, you must take Ruth, the Moabite woman, also. She is the wife of the dead man. You must keep alive the name of the dead man on his land." ⁶Then the close in-law said, ". . . Take it for yourself. I give you my right to buy it, for I cannot buy it." . . .

¹³So Boaz took Ruth. She became his wife. . . . The Lord made it possible for her to have a child and she gave birth to a son. . . . ¹⁷The neighbor women gave him a name. They said, "A son has been born to Naomi!" And they called him Obed. He is the father of Jesse, the father of David.

Kid-Builder Value

LOYALTY is strong devotion to a person or ideal. Ruth showed loyalty to Naomi by leaving her people and going to Naomi's land.

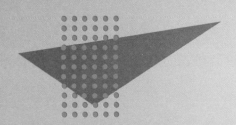

KID-BUILDER Questions

- How did Ruth help Naomi?

- What good things happened to Ruth because of her loyalty?

- How do you show loyalty to your friends? How do they show loyalty to you?

- How do you feel when your friends are loyal? Has there been a time when someone wasn't loyal to you? What happened?

KID-BUILDER Prayer

Lord, help me be loyal to my friends and family and to You always.   In Jesus' name. Amen.

Memory Verse:
A man who has friends must be a friend, but there is a friend who stays nearer than a brother.   Prov. 18:24

I Samuel

The fourth book of history is *I Samuel* (SAM-you-ull), which tells the history of the Israelites from the birth of Samuel to the death of King Saul. The period of the judges is about to end. Samuel, a judge, prophet, and priest is the last of the judges. Although the book is named after Samuel, no one knows for sure who wrote it. The book is filled with stories of Samuel, David, and Saul. You might recognize some of the ones that follow.

II Samuel

Second Samuel tells what happens during David's reign as king. Even though David is a great king, he makes some bad choices: David plots the death of Uriah so that he can marry Uriah's wife Bathsheba, and David orders a census of his army so that he can brag about how powerful it is. God is not pleased with these choices, and David must face the consequences for not obeying God. Because he is quick to ask God to forgive him, David is known as a man "after God's own heart."

I SAMUEL

Hannah Is Prayerful

I Samuel 1

There was a . . . man . . . of the hill country of Ephraim. His name was Elkanah. . . . ²He had two wives. The name of one was Hannah. The name of the other was Peninnah. Peninnah had children, but Hannah had no children. ³This man would go from his city each year to worship and to give gifts on the altar in Shiloh to the Lord. . . . Eli's two sons, Hophni and Phinehas, were the Lord's religious leaders there. ⁴On the day when Elkanah killed animals on the altar in worship, he would give part of the gift to his wife Peninnah and to all her sons and daughters. ⁵But he would give twice as much to Hannah, for he loved Hannah. But the Lord had made it so she could not have children. ⁶Peninnah would try to make her very angry,

Kid-Builder Fact
I Sam. 1:5 In Bible times, most men and women were very sad when they were unable to have children. They thought God was punishing them by withholding children from them.

because the Lord would not let her have children. [7]So it happened, year after year, each time Hannah went up to the house of the Lord, Peninnah would make her angry. Hannah cried and would not eat. [8]Then her husband Elkanah said to her, "Hannah, why are you crying? . . . Am I not better to you than ten sons? . . ."

Eli the religious leader was sitting on the seat by the door of the house of the Lord. [10]Hannah was very troubled. She prayed to the Lord and cried with sorrow. 11Then she made a promise and said, "O Lord of All, . . . remember me. Do not forget Your woman servant, but give me a son. If You will, then I will give him to the Lord all his life. And no hair will ever be cut from his head."

12While she kept praying to the Lord, Eli was watching her mouth. 13Hannah was speaking in her heart. Her lips were moving, but her voice was not heard. So Eli thought she had drunk too much. 14Eli said to her, "How long will you be drunk? Put wine away from you." 15But Hannah answered, "No, my lord, I am a woman troubled in spirit. I have not drunk wine or strong drink, but I was pouring out my soul to the Lord. 16Do not think of your woman servant as a woman of no worth. For I have been speaking out of much trouble and pain in my spirit." 17Then Eli answered, "Go in peace. May the God of Israel do what you have asked of Him." 18And Hannah said, "Let your woman servant find favor in your eyes." So she went her way and ate, and her face was no longer sad.

19The family got up early in the morning and worshiped before the Lord. Then they returned to their house in Ramah. . . . 20The Lord made it pos-

Kid-Builder Value
PRAYERFULNESS is regular participation in prayer. Hannah showed this quality when she poured out her heart to God.

sible for [Hannah] to have a child, and when the time came she gave birth to a son. She gave him the name Samuel, saying, "I have asked the Lord for him."

²¹Then Elkanah went up with all those of his house to give the Lord the gift on the altar in worship as he did each year, and to pay what he had promised. ²²But Hannah did not go. For she said to her husband, "I will not go up until the child no longer needs to be nursed. Then I will bring him before the Lord, to stay there forever." ²³Elkanah . . . said to her, "Do what you think is best. . . ." ²⁴When she had finished nursing him, she took him with her to the house of the Lord in Shiloh. . . . ²⁵She brought a three year old bull, one basket of flour and a jar of wine also. Then they killed the bull, and brought the boy to Eli. ²⁶Hannah said, "O, my lord! As you live, my lord, I am the woman who stood here beside you, praying to the Lord. ²⁷I prayed for this boy, and the Lord has given me what I asked of Him. ²⁸So I have given him to the Lord. He is given to the Lord as long as he lives." And they worshiped the Lord there.

Kid-Builder Fact
I Sam. 1:3 Eli was both judge and high priest of Israel for forty years. He lived at Shiloh, near the tabernacle.

KID-BUILDER Questions

- For what did Hannah pray?

- How was her prayer answered?

- Hannah kept praying because she had faith that God would answer. How is prayerfulness a good quality to have when you're facing hard times?

- Are there times when you seek God more than others? What are those times?

KID-BUILDER Prayer

Lord, I want to be prayerful like Hannah was. Help me be faithful in prayer.   In Jesus' name. Amen.

Memory Verse:
I did not give up waiting for the Lord. And He turned to me and heard my cry.   Ps. 40:1

The Lord Calls Samuel

I Samuel 3

The boy Samuel was working for the Lord with Eli. There were few words from the Lord given in those days, and there were not many special dreams. ²At that time Eli was lying down in his own place. His eyes had become weak and he could not see well. ³. . . Samuel was lying down in the house of the Lord where the special box of God was. ⁴Then the Lord called Samuel, and Samuel said, "Here I am." ⁵He ran to Eli and said, "Here I am, for you called me." But Eli said, "I did not call you. Lie down again." So Samuel went and lay down. ⁶The Lord called again, "Samuel!" So Samuel got up and went to Eli, and said, "Here I am, for you called me." But Eli answered, "I did not call you, my son. Lie down again." ⁷Now Samuel did not

Kid-Builder Value
RESPECTFULNESS is an attitude of high regard for someone. Eli encouraged Samuel to be respectful when answering the Lord's call.

know the Lord yet. . . .
⁸The Lord called Samuel again for the third time. He got up and went to Eli, and said, "Here I am, for you called me." Then Eli understood that the Lord was calling the boy. ⁹Eli said to Samuel, "Go lie down. If He calls you, say, 'Speak, Lord, for Your servant is listening.'" So Samuel went and lay down in his place.

¹⁰Then the Lord came and stood and called as He did the other times, "Samuel! Samuel!" And Samuel said, "Speak, for Your servant is listening." ¹¹The Lord said to Samuel, "See, I am about to do a thing in Israel which will make both ears of everyone who hears it feel strange. ¹²On that day I will do all I have said against the family of Eli. ¹³I have told him that I will punish his family forever for the sin he knew about. Because his sons brought the sin upon themselves, and Eli did not stop them. ¹⁴So I swear to the family of Eli that the sin of his family will not be paid for with

gifts given on the altar forever."

15Samuel lay down until morning. Then he opened the doors of the house of the Lord. But Samuel was afraid to tell Eli about the special dream. 16Eli called Samuel and said, "Samuel, my son." And Samuel said, "Here I am." 17Eli said, "What did the Lord tell you? Do not hide it from me. May God do so to you and more, if you hide anything from me of all He said to you." 18So Samuel told him everything and hid nothing from him. And Eli said, "It is the Lord. Let him do what is good in His eyes."

19Samuel grew. And the Lord was with him and made everything he said come true. 20All Israel from Dan to Beersheba knew that Samuel had become a man of God.

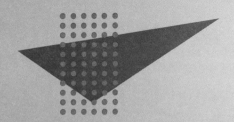

KID-BUILDER Questions

- Samuel heard someone call his name. Who did he think called him?

- When your parents call you, how do you answer? How do you answer when your friends call? Is there a difference between how you talk to your parents and how you talk to your friends?

- Who or what have you been taught to respect? Why is respect important?

KID-BUILDER Prayer

Lord, You deserve my respect and praise. Teach me to respect Your Word, as well as the people who are in authority over me.   *In Jesus' name. Amen.*

Memory Verse:
Show respect to all men. Love the Christians. Honor God with love and fear.   I Pet. 2:17a

I SAMUEL

David and Goliath

I Samuel 17

Once more the Philistines tried to make trouble for Israel. This time they had a giant named Goliath with them. For forty days, Goliath tried to scare the Israelites. Israel needed a champion too. . . .

The Philistines gathered their armies for battle. . . . ²Saul and the men of Israel were gathered together, and set up their tents in the valley of Elah. . . . ³The Philistines stood on the mountain on one side while Israel stood on the mountain on the other side, with the valley between them. ⁴Then a strong fighter came out from the armies of the Philistines. His name was Goliath, from Gath. He was almost twice as tall as most men. ⁵He had a head covering of brass, and wore brass battle-clothes that weighed as much as 5000 silver pieces. ⁶He wore brass leg-coverings, and had a brass spear on his shoulders. ⁷. . .The iron head of his spear weighed as much as 600 pieces of silver. A man walked before him to carry his shield. ⁸Goliath stood and called out to the army of Israel, saying, ". . . Choose a man for yourselves, and let him come down to me. 9If he is able to fight with me and kill me, then we will be your servants. But if I fight him and kill him, then you must become our servants and work for us." . . . 11When Saul and all Israel heard these words of the Philistine, they were troubled. . . .

12Now David was the [youngest] son of Jesse . . . of Bethlehem in Judah. Jesse had eight sons. . . . 13Jesse's three older sons had followed Saul to the battle. . . .

17Jesse said to . . . David, "Take for your brothers a basket of this baked grain and these ten loaves. . . . See how your brothers are doing, and bring me news of them. . . ."

20So David got up early in the morning and left the flock in the care of a shepherd. . . . 22David . . . went to meet with his brothers. 23As he talked with them, Goliath . . . came out . . . and spoke the same words as before. . . . 24When all the men of Israel saw the man, they . . . were very much afraid. . . .

26Then David said to the men standing by him, ". . . Who is this Philistine . . . that he should make fun of the armies of the living God?" . . .

31When David's words were heard, they were

Kid-Builder Value
CONFIDENCE is a feeling of security based on faith and trust. David had confidence that the Lord would help him defeat Goliath.

told to Saul, and Saul sent for him. 32David said to Saul, ". . . Your servant will go and fight with this Philistine." 33Saul said to David, ". . . You are only a young man, while he has been a man of war since he was young." 34But David said to Saul, "Your servant was taking care of his father's sheep. When a lion or a bear came and took a lamb from the flock, 35I went after him and fought him and saved it from his mouth. . . . 36Your servant has killed both the lion and the bear. . . . [T]his Philistine . . . will be like one of them. For he has made fun of the armies of the living God. . . . 37The Lord . . . will save me from the hand of this Philistine." Saul said to David, "Go, and may the Lord be with you." 38Then Saul dressed David with his clothes. He put a brass head covering on his head, and dressed him with heavy battle-clothes.

39David put on his sword over his heavy battle-clothes and tried to walk. . . . Then David said to Saul, "I cannot go with these, for I am not used to them." And David took them off. 40He took his stick in his hand, and chose five smooth stones from the river. He put them in his shepherd's bag. His [sling] was in his hand, and he went to the Philistine. . . .

42When the Philistine looked and saw David, he thought nothing of him. For he was only a young man, with good color in his skin, and good looking. 43The Philistine said to David, "Am I a dog, that you come to me with sticks?" And the Philistine spoke against David by his gods. . . . 45Then David said to the Philistine, "You come to me with a sword and spears. But I come to you in the name of the Lord of All, the God of the armies of Israel, Whom you have stood against. 46This day the Lord will give you into my hands. . . . 47All these people gathered here may know that the Lord does not save with sword and spear. For the battle is the Lord's and He will give you into our hands." 48Then the Philistine rose up and came to meet David. And David rushed to the center of the valley to meet the Philistine. 49David put his hand into his bag, took out a stone and threw it, and hit the Philistine on his forehead. The stone went into his forehead, so that he fell on his face to the ground.

50So David won the fight against the Philistine with a [sling] and a stone. He hit the Philistine and killed him. There was no sword in David's hand.

51. . . When the Philistines saw that their strong soldier was dead, they ran away.

Kid-Builder Fact

I Sam. 7:40 A *sling* was a weapon carried by shepherds to throw stones at animals attacking their flocks. Slings were sometimes used by soldiers. The sling was made of two narrow strips of leather joined in the middle by a wider piece where the stone was held. The shepherd tied one end to his wrist. The other end was held in his hand. The sling was then skillfully swung around and the loose end released to make the stone fly.

KID-BUILDER Questions

- Describe Goliath. What threat did he make?

- David could not have defeated Goliath if he had not had confidence in the Lord's ability to fight for him. There are giants we face today. These are problems such as hard subjects at school, loneliness, etc. What giants are you facing?

- How can remembering how God helped David give you confidence to face the giants in your life?

KID-BUILDER Prayer

Lord, I need Your help each day. When the giants come my way, I want to be victorious like David.
                              In Jesus' name. Amen.

Memory Verse:
For the battle is not yours but God's.   II Chron. 20:15b

HISTORY

I and II Kings

First and II Kings tell the story of Israel's kings, beginning with Solomon's crowning as king of Israel. It also tells how he builds a temple for the Lord.

When Solomon sins against God, however, the kingdom of Israel is divided into two kingdoms—the northern kingdom (Israel) and the southern kingdom (Judah). Many kings from both kingdoms disobey God.

Several prophets warn the kings of God's judgment. Among them are Elijah and Elisha, who demonstrate God's power through many miracles.

I and II Chronicles

First and II Chronicles (KRON-uh-culls) cover some of the same events concerning Israel's kings as II Samuel, and I and II Kings. However, they concentrate more on Judah than on Israel, and tell more about the religious history and the temple.

Because of disobedience, God's judgment eventually falls on both kingdoms. The northern kingdom is taken captive by Assyria in 722 B.C. and the southern kingdom is taken captive by Babylon in 586 B.C. The great temple that Solomon built is left in ruins.

I KINGS

Solomon Becomes King

I Kings 1—3

Now King David was old. He had lived many years. . . .

²⁹The king made a promise and said, "As the Lord lives, Who has saved me from all trouble, ³⁰I promised you by the Lord the God of Israel, saying, '. . . Solomon will be king after me. . . .'"

²:¹⁰Then David died and was buried in the city of David. ¹¹He had ruled over Israel forty years. . . . ¹²Solomon sat on the throne of his father David and things went well for the nation.

³:³Now Solomon loved the Lord. He walked in the Laws of his father David. . . . ⁵The Lord came to Solomon in a special dream in Gibeon during the night. God said, "Ask what you wish Me to give you." ⁶Then Solomon said, "You have shown great loving-kindness to Your servant David my father because he was faithful and . . . pure in heart before You. . . . ⁷Now, O Lord my God, You have made Your servant king in place of my father David. But I am only a little child. I do not know

how to start or finish. . . . ⁹So give Your servant an understanding heart to judge Your people and know the difference between good and bad. For who is able to judge Your many people?"

¹⁰It pleased the Lord that Solomon had asked this. ¹¹God said to him, "You have asked this, and have not asked for a long life for yourself. You have not asked for riches, or for the life of those who hate you. . . . Because you have asked this, ¹²I have done what you said. See, I have given you a wise and understanding heart. No one has been like you before, and there will be no one like you in the future. ¹³I give you what you have not asked, also. I give you both riches and honor. So there will be no king like you all your days. ¹⁴And if you walk in My ways and keep My Laws and Word as your father David did, I will allow you to live a long time."

¹⁵Solomon awoke, and saw it was a dream. . . .

¹⁶Then two women . . . came to the king and stood in front of him. ¹⁷One of the women said, "O my lord, this woman and I live in the same house. And I gave birth to a child while she was in the house. ¹⁸On the third day after I gave birth, this

Kid-Builder Value
WISDOM includes knowledge of facts, skills, common sense, good judgment, and godly living. King Solomon was considered the wisest man who ever lived.

woman gave birth to a child also. And we were alone. There was no one else with us in the house. . . . 19This woman's son died during the night. . . . 20So she got up in the night and took my son from my side while I was asleep. She laid him in her arms, and her dead son in my arms. 21When I got up in the morning to nurse my son, I saw that he was dead. But when I came nearer and looked, I saw that he was not my son who was born to me." 22Then the other woman said, "No! The living one is my son, and the dead one is your son." But the first woman said, "No! The dead one is your son and the living one is my son." They spoke this way in front of the king. . . .

24And the king said, "Bring me a sword." So they brought a sword to the king. 25And the king said, "Divide the living child in two. Give half to the one woman and half to the other." 26Then the mother of the living child had much pity for her son and said to the king, "O, my lord, give her the living child. Do not kill him." But the other woman said, "He will not be mine or yours. Divide him." 27Then the king answered and said, "Give the first woman the living child. Do not kill him. She is his mother." 28When all Israel heard how the king had decided, they were afraid of him. For they saw that the wisdom of God was in him, to do what is right and fair.

KID-BUILDER Questions

- What was Solomon's decision when two women brought the child to him? How was his decision wise?

- Have you ever asked God for wisdom? How has wisdom helped you?

- Have you ever made an unwise choice? What happened? What could you have done differently in that situation?

KID-BUILDER Prayer

Lord, the Bible says wisdom comes from You. Please give me wisdom to make choices that please You.
In Jesus' name. Amen.

Memory Verse:
The fear of the Lord is the beginning of much learning.   Prov. 1:7a

I KINGS

Elijah on Mount Carmel

I Kings 18

After Solomon's death, the kingdom of Israel split into two kingdoms: Israel and Judah. Ahab was the king of Israel. He did sinful things, which displeased God. He sent Ahab a message through His prophet Elijah.

The word of the Lord came to Elijah, in the third year, saying, "Go show yourself to Ahab. And I will send rain upon the earth." . . .

¹⁷When he saw Elijah, Ahab said to him, "Is it you, the one who brings trouble to Israel?" ¹⁸Elijah said, "I have not brought trouble to Israel. But you and your father's house have. Because you have turned away from the laws of the Lord, and have followed the false gods of Baal. ¹⁹So now call together all Israel to me at Mount Carmel. And gather together 450 men who speak for Baal and 400 men who speak for the false goddess Asherah, who eat at Jezebel's table."

²⁰So Ahab sent news among all the people of Israel. And he brought the men who speak for the

false gods together at Mount Carmel. ²¹Elijah came near all the people and said, "How long will you be divided between two ways of thinking? If the Lord is God, follow Him. But if Baal is God, then follow him." But the people did not answer him a word. ²²Then Elijah said to the people . . . ²³"Bring two bulls to us. Let them choose one bull for themselves and cut it up and put it on the wood. But put no fire under it. I will make the other bull ready and lay it on the wood. And I will put no fire under it. ²⁴Then you call on the name of your god, and I will call on the name of the Lord. The God Who answers by fire, He is God." All the people answered and said, "That is a good idea."

²⁵So Elijah said to the men who spoke for Baal, "Choose one bull for yourselves. . . . Then call on the name of your god. . . ." ²⁶So they took the bull . . . and made it ready. Then they called on the name of Baal from morning until noon, saying, "O Baal, answer us." But there was no voice. No one answered. They jumped and danced around the altar they had made. ²⁷At noon Elijah made fun of them. He said, "Call out with a loud voice. . . . It might be that he is in deep thought or has turned away. He could be away traveling. Or it may be that he is asleep and needs to have someone wake him." ²⁸So they cried with a loud voice. They cut themselves as they had done in the past, with swords and spears until blood poured out on them.

²⁹When noon passed, they cried out until the time for giving the evening gift. . . . No one answered. . . .

³⁰Then Elijah said to all the people, "Come near to me." So all the people came near to him. And he built again the altar of the Lord which had been torn down. ³¹Then Elijah took twelve stones, by the

number of the families of Jacob's sons. . . . [32]With the stones he built an altar in the name of the Lord. And he made a ditch around the altar. . . . [33]Then he set the wood in place. He cut the bull in pieces and laid it on the wood. And he said, "Fill four jars with water and pour it on the burnt gift and on the wood." [34]Then he said, "Do it a second time." And they did it a second time. He said, "Do it a third time." And they did it a third time. [35]The water flowed around the altar, and filled the ditch also. [36]Then the time came for giving the evening gift. Elijah . . . came near and said, "O Lord, God of Abraham, Isaac and Israel, let it be known today that You are God in Israel. Let it be known that I am Your servant, and have done all these things at Your word. [37]Answer me, O Lord. Answer me so these people may know that You, O Lord, are God. Turn their hearts to You again." [38]Then the fire of the Lord fell. It burned up the burnt gift, the wood, the stones and the dust. And it picked up the water that was in the ditch. [39]All the people fell on their faces when they saw it. They said, "The Lord, He is

Kid-Builder Fact
I Kings 18:19 *Baal* was the name of many gods worshiped by the people of Canaan. They thought the Baal gods ruled their land, crops, and animals. The Canaanites believed that each year Baal had a battle with the sea and rivers, bringing them under his power. Baal then made it rain on the fields for a good crop. The Canaanites made images or idols of Baal.

God. The Lord, He is God." ⁴⁰Then Elijah said to them, "Take hold of the men who speak for Baal. Do not let one of them get away." So they took hold of them. And Elijah brought them down to the river Kishon, and killed them there.

⁴¹Then Elijah said to Ahab, "Go up, eat and drink. For there is the sound of much rain." ⁴²So Ahab went. . . . But Elijah went up to the top of Carmel. He got down on the ground and put his face between his knees. ⁴³And he said to his servant, "Go up now and look toward the sea." So he went up and looked and said, "There is nothing." Seven times Elijah said, "Go again." ⁴⁴The seventh time, he said, "I see a cloud as small as a man's hand coming up from the sea." Elijah said, "Go and tell Ahab, 'Make your war-wagon ready and go down, so that the rain does not stop you.' " ⁴⁵Soon the sky became black with clouds and wind, and there was much rain. And Ahab went to Jezreel. ⁴⁶Then the hand of the Lord was on Elijah. He pulled his clothing up under his belt and ran before Ahab to Jezreel.

Kid-Builder Value
CONFIDENCE is a feeling of security based on faith and trust. Elijah had confidence in the true God, not the false god Baal.

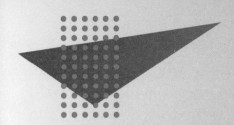

KID-BUILDER Questions

- How did Elijah show confidence in God?

- Who won the challenge between God and Baal? Who did the people believe in?

- There may be times when you will be challenged about your beliefs in God. How can you show confidence in Him?

- Elijah knew the real God. Do you? What do you know about Him?

KID-BUILDER Prayer

Lord, thank You for being with me always. Help me remember to put my trust in You.

In Jesus' name. Amen.

Memory Verse

The Lord is my light and the One Who saves me. Whom should I fear? The Lord is the strength of my life. Of whom should I be afraid?   Ps. 27:1

II KINGS

Elisha Becomes God's Prophet

II Kings 2

When the Lord was about to take Elijah up to heaven by a wind-storm, Elijah and Elisha were on their way from Gilgal. 2Elijah said to Elisha, "Stay here, I ask you. For the Lord has sent me as far as Bethel." But Elisha said, "As the Lord lives and as you yourself live, I will not leave you." So they went down to Bethel. 3Then the sons of the men who spoke for God at Bethel came out to Elisha. They said to him, "Do you know that the Lord will take Elijah from you today?" And he said, "Yes, I know. Say no more." 4Elijah said to him, "Elisha, I ask you to stay here. For the Lord has sent me to Jericho." But Elisha said, "As the Lord lives and as you yourself live, I will not leave you." So they came to Jericho. 5The sons of the men who spoke for God at Jericho came to Elisha. They said to him, "Do you know that the Lord will take Elijah from you today?" And he answered, "Yes, I know. Say no more." 6Then Elijah said to him, "I ask you to stay here. For the Lord has sent me to the

Jordan." And Elisha said, "As the Lord lives and as you yourself live, I will not leave you." So the two of them went on. . . .

⁸Then Elijah took his coat and rolled it up and hit the water. And the water divided,. . . so the two of them crossed the Jordan on dry ground. ⁹When they had crossed, Elijah said to Elisha, "Ask what I should do for you before I am taken from you." And Elisha said, "I ask you, let twice the share of your spirit be upon me." ¹⁰Elijah said, "You have asked a hard thing. But if you see me when I am taken from you, it will be given to you. But if not, it will not be so." ¹¹As they went on and talked, a [chariot] of fire and horses of fire came between them. And Elijah went up by a wind-storm to heaven. ¹²Elisha saw it and cried out, "My father, my father, the [chariot] of Israel and its horsemen!" And he saw Elijah no more.Then he . . . tore [his own clothes] in two pieces. ¹³He picked up Elijah's coat that had fallen from him. And he returned and stood by the side of the Jordan. ¹⁴He took Elijah's coat that fell from him, and hit the water and said, "Where is the Lord, the God of Elijah? "When he hit the water, it was divided, . . . and Elisha crossed the Jordan.

Kid-Builder Value
DEDICATION is a complete commitment to something or someone. Elisha was dedicated to serving the Lord and Elijah. We can show our dedication by our actions.

KID-BUILDER Questions

- Each time Elijah told Elisha to stay behind, what did Elisha tell him?

- What happened to Elijah? What happened to his coat?

- Elisha was ready to carry on Elijah's work. His asking for a double portion of Elijah's spiritual power meant he was dedicated to the task. What are some ways that you can show God that you are dedicated to serving Him?

KID-BUILDER Prayer

Lord, help me be dedicated like Elisha and Elijah.
In Jesus' name. Amen.

Memory Verse:
I have fought a good fight. I have finished the work I was to do. I have kept the faith.   II Tim. 4:7

Naaman Is Healed

II Kings 5

Naaman the captain of the army of the king of Syria was an important man to his king. He was much respected, because by him the Lord had made Syria win in battle. Naaman was a strong man of war, but he had a bad skin disease. 2Now the Syrians had gone out in groups of soldiers, and had taken a little girl from the land of Israel. She served Naaman's wife. 3And she said to her owner, "I wish that my owner's husband were with the man of God who is in Samaria! Then he would heal his bad skin disease." 4So Naaman went in and told his king, "This is what the girl from the land of Israel said." 5The king of Syria said, "Go now, and I will send a letter to the king of Israel." So Naaman went and took with him silver weighing as much as ten men, 6000 pieces of gold, and ten changes of clothes. 6He brought the letter to the king of Israel, which said, "I have sent my servant Naaman to you with this letter, that you may heal his bad skin disease." 7When the king of Israel read the letter, he tore his clothes and said, "Am I God, to kill and to make alive? Is this why this man sends word to me to heal a man's bad skin disease? Think about it. He wants to start a fight with me."

8Elisha the man of God heard that the king of Israel had torn his clothes. So he sent word to the king, saying, "Why have you torn your clothes? Let him come to me. Then he will know that there is a man of God in Israel." 9So Naaman came with his horses and his [chariots], and stood at the door of Elisha's house. 10Elisha sent a man to him, saying, "Go and wash in the Jordan seven times. And your flesh will be made well and you will be clean." 11But Naaman was very angry and went away. He said, "I thought he would come out to me, and stand, and call on the name of the Lord his God. I thought he would wave his hand over the place, and heal the bad skin disease. 12Are not Abanah and Pharpar, the rivers of Damascus, better than all the waters of Israel? Could I not wash in them and be clean?" So he turned and went away very angry. 13Then his servants came and said to him, "My father, if the man of God had told you to do some great thing, would you not have done it? How much more then, when he says to you, 'Wash and be clean'?" 14So Naaman went down into the Jordan River seven times, as the man of God had told him. And his flesh was made as well as the flesh of a little child. He was clean.

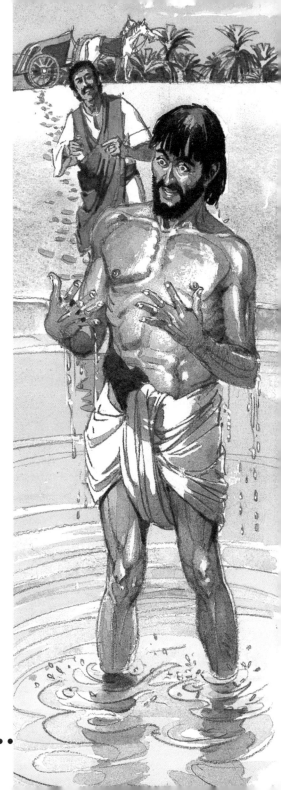

¹⁵Then Naaman returned to the man of God with all those who were with him. He came and stood in front of Elisha and said, "See, now I know that there is no God in all the earth but in Israel. So I ask you now to take a gift from your servant." ¹⁶But Elisha said, "As the Lord lives, before Whom I stand, I will take nothing." Naaman tried to talk him into taking it, but he would not. . . . ¹⁹And Elisha said to him, "Go in peace." So Naaman went away from him a short way.

²⁰But Gehazi, the servant of Elisha

the man of God, thought, "See, my owner has let Naaman the Syrian go without receiving the gift he brought. As the Lord lives, I will run after him and take something from him." 21So Gehazi went after Naaman. When Naaman saw someone running after him, he stepped off the [chariot] to meet him, and said, "Is all well?" 22Gehazi said, "All is well. My owner has sent me, saying, 'See, just now two young sons of the men who tell what will happen in the future have come to me from the hill country of Ephraim. I ask of you, give them a man's weight in silver and two changes of clothes.' " 23Naaman said, "Be pleased to take silver weighing as much as two men." And he had him take two bags of silver weighing as much as two men, with two changes of clothes. . . .

25And Gehazi went in and stood in front of his owner. Elisha said to him, "Where have you been, Gehazi?" And he said, "Your servant did not leave." 26Elisha said to him, "Did I not go with you in spirit when the man turned from his [chariot] to meet you? Was it a time to receive

Kid-Builder Fact
II Kings 5:10 The Jordan River was the most important river in Israel's history. It begins in the mountains north of the Sea of Galilee, runs into the Sea of Galilee, then out and down to the Dead Sea, where it ends. Because it is so winding, it travels about 200 miles to cover its 65-mile route.

money and clothes and olive fields and grape fields and sheep and cattle and men servants and women servants? 27So now the bad skin disease will be upon you and your children forever." And Gehazi went away from Elisha with a bad skin disease. He was as white as snow.

Kid-Builder Value
OBEDIENCE is doing what you're instructed to do. Naaman learned to submit and obey God's plan in order to be healed.

KID-BUILDER Questions

- Who told Naaman about Elisha?

- What was Elisha's advice? How did Naaman react? What finally happened when Naaman obeyed?

- Washing in the muddy Jordan was an insult to Naaman's pride. Was there a time when you were afraid to obey because you thought you would look bad? What happened?

- Sometimes obeying God comes at the risk of being embarrassed. Which is better—to obey God or to look good in front of your friends? Why?

KID-BUILDER Prayer

Lord, help me be obedient and not be concerned about my own pride or looking foolish.

In Jesus' name. Amen.

Memory Verse:
Pride comes before being destroyed and a proud spirit comes before a fall.   Prov. 16:18

II CHRONICLES

God Helps Jehoshaphat

II Chronicles 17, 20

The Lord was with Jehoshaphat because he followed the early ways of his father. He did not follow the false gods of Baal. ⁴He looked to the God of his father, followed His Laws, and did not act as Israel did. ⁵So the Lord made the nation strong under his rule. And all Judah paid taxes to Jehoshaphat. He had great riches and honor. ⁶He was strong in his heart in the ways of the Lord....

20:1After this the men of Moab, and Ammon, and some of the Meunites, came to make war against Jehoshaphat. . . . ³Jehoshaphat was afraid and decided to call on the Lord. He made a special time of not eating in all Judah. ⁴And Judah gathered together to pray for help from the Lord....

⁵Jehoshaphat stood among the people of Judah and Jerusalem, in the house of the Lord.... ⁶Then he said, "O Lord, the God of our fathers, are You not God in heaven? Do You not rule over all the nations? Power and strength are in Your hand, so that no one is able to stand against You. ⁷O our

God, did You not make the people of this land leave so that Your people Israel could have it and give it to the children of Your friend Abraham forever? 8And they have lived in it. . . . 10Now see the men of Ammon and Moab and Mount Seir, whom You did not let Israel fight when they came from the land of Egypt. (They turned aside from them and did not destroy them.) 11Look how they are paying us back. They are coming to make us leave Your land which You have given to us. 12O our God, will You not punish them? For we have no power against all these men who are coming against us. We do not know what to do. But our eyes look to You." . . .

14Then the Spirit of the Lord came upon Jahaziel the son of Zechariah . . . as he stood among the people. 15He said, "Listen, all Judah, the people of Jerusalem, and King Jehoshaphat. The Lord says to you "Do not be afraid or troubled because of these many men. For the battle is not yours but God's. . . . 17You will not need to fight in this battle. Just stand still in your places and see the saving power of the Lord work for you, O Judah and Jerusalem.' . . . Go out against them tomorrow, for

Kid-Builder Fact
II Chron. 17:1 Jehoshaphat was one of the most powerful kings of Judah. He had wealth, many troops, and cities. He reigned for twenty-five years. The Lord gave Jehoshaphat's kingdom peace from its enemies.

the Lord is with you." [18]Then Jehoshaphat put his face to the ground. And all Judah and the people of Jerusalem fell down in worship before the Lord. . . .

[20]They got up early in the morning and went out to the desert of Tekoa. When they went out, Jehoshaphat stood and said, "Listen to me, O Judah and people of Jerusalem. Trust in the Lord your God, and you will be made strong. Trust in the men who speak for Him, and you will do well." [21]When he had spoken with the people, he called those who sang to the Lord and those who praised Him in holy clothing. They went out in front of the army and said, "Give thanks to the Lord. For His loving-kindness lasts forever." [22]When they began

²¹When he had spoken with the people, he called those who sang to the Lord and those who praised Him in holy clothing. They went out in front of the army and said, "Give thanks to the Lord. For His loving-kindness lasts forever." ²²When they began to sing and praise, the Lord set traps against the men of Ammon, Moab, and Mount Seir, who had come against Judah. So they were destroyed. ²³The men of Ammon and Moab fought against the people of Mount Seir, and killed all of them. And when they finished with the people of Seir, they all helped to kill each other.

²⁴Judah came to the place where they could look out over the desert. . . . [T]hey saw that dead bodies were lying on the ground. No one had been left alive. . . . ²⁶They . . . praised and thanked the Lord. So the name of that place has been the Valley of Beracah to this day. ²⁷Then every man of Judah and Jerusalem returned, with Jehoshaphat leading them. They returned to Jerusalem with joy. For the Lord had filled them with joy by saving them from those who hated them.

Kid-Builder Value
PRAISE includes words or actions that give honor to someone. Jehoshaphat and the people offered praise to God after He helped them.

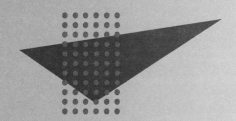

KID-BUILDER Questions

- What bad news did Jehoshaphat receive? What did he do?

- What did Jehoshaphat and the people do to celebrate their victory? When something good happens to you, who gets the glory?

- Name a new way you'd like to praise God.

KID-BUILDER Prayer

Dear Lord, help me praise You with my whole life.
In Jesus' name. Amen.

Memory Verse:
Let us honor and thank the God and Father of our Lord Jesus Christ. He has already given us a taste of what heaven is like.

Eph. 1:3

HISTORY

Ezra

The Book of *Ezra* (EZ-ruh) continues the story of II Chronicles and tells about the Jewish people returning to Jerusalem after the Babylon captivity. Ezra is a priest, scribe, and scholar who helps his people worship God again.

Nehemiah

Nehemiah (NEE-huh-MY-uh) tells the story of rebuilding the walls of Jerusalem. Nehemiah is a good organizer. He orders the supplies and supervises the work on the wall. The people trust him and work hard to complete the work in fifty-two days. When the construction is completed, Nehemiah calls the people to worship God.

Esther

The Book of *Esther* (ES-ter) takes place during the Jewish exile in Persia. Esther, an orphaned Jewish girl, becomes Queen of Persia and risks her life to save her people. She is obedient to her cousin Mordecai, and God uses her to change the fate of a nation. We learn through this story that God is in control of all that happens in history.

NEHEMIAH

Nehemiah Rebuilds the Wall

Nehemiah 1—8

Because of their sin, God had allowed His people to be captured by their enemies. They were forced to leave their land and live in Babylon. Nehemiah, the cupbearer of a king, was the leader of the third group of Jewish exiles who returned to live in Jerusalem.

These are the words of Nehemiah. . . . While I was in the king's house in Susa, ²Hanani, one of my brothers, and some men from Judah came. I asked them about the Jews who were still living and had gotten away from Babylon, and about Jerusalem. ³They said to me, "The Jews who are left who have returned to the land from Babylon are in much trouble and shame. The wall of Jerusalem is broken down and its gates are destroyed by fire."

⁴When I heard this, I sat down and cried and was filled with sorrow for days. I did not eat, and I prayed to the God of heaven. . . .

²:¹. . . I took up the wine and gave it to the king. . . . ²So the king said to me, "Why is your face so

sad when you are not sick? It must be that you are sad in your heart." Then I was very much afraid. . . . 4Then the king said to me, "What are you asking for?" So I prayed to the God of heaven. 5And I said to the king, "If it pleases the king, . . . send me to Judah, to the city of my fathers' graves. Let me build it again." . . . So it pleased the king to send me. . . . 7And I said to the king, "If it please the king, let letters be given to me for the leaders of the lands on the other side of the River, that they may allow me to pass through until I come to Judah." 8. . . And the king gave me what I asked for, because the good hand of my God was upon me. . . .

11I came to Jerusalem and was there for three days. 12Then I got up in the night, I and a few men with me. I did not tell anyone what my God was putting into my mind to do for Jerusalem. . . . 13I went out at night by the Valley Gate to the Dragon's Well and to the Waste Gate. I looked at the walls of Jerusalem which were broken down and its gates which were destroyed by fire. . . . 16The leaders did not know where I had

Kid-Builder Fact
Joshua 6:1 Walls in Bible times were the major way of defending cities against attack. Every ancient city had huge walls made of mud, stones, or brick. Some of these walls are still standing today. Joshua 6:4 The religious leaders were called priests.

gone or what I had done. .
. . ¹⁷Then I said to them,
"You see the problem we
have. Jerusalem lies
waste and its gates
are destroyed by fire.
Come, let us build
the wall of Jerusalem
again, that we may no
longer be put to
shame." . . . So they
put their hands to the
good work. . . .

⁴:⁷When Sanballat,
Tobiah, the Arabs,
the Ammonites and
the Ashdodites heard
that the work of
building the walls of
Jerusalem went on, and
that the broken places
began to be closed, they
were very angry. ⁸And
all of them made
plans together to
come and fight against
Jerusalem and cause
trouble in it. ⁹But we
prayed to our God

because of them. And we had men watching for them day and night. . . .

¹²When the Jews who lived by them came, they told us ten times, "They will come up against us from all the places where they live.". . . ¹⁴When I saw their fear, I got up and said to the rulers and leaders and the rest of the people, "Do not be afraid of them. Remember the Lord Who is great and honored with fear. And fight for your brothers, your sons, your daughters, your wives, and your houses.". . .

¹⁶From that day on, half of my servants did the work while half of them held the spears, battle-coverings, bows, and battle-clothes. And the captains stood behind the whole house of Judah. ¹⁷Those who were building the wall and those who carried loads did their work with one hand, and held something to fight with in the other hand. . . .

⁶:¹It was told to Sanballat, Tobiah, Geshem the Arab, and to the rest of those who hated us that I had built the wall again. They were told that the wall had no more open places, but I had not yet set up the doors in the gates. ²So Sanballat and Geshem sent word to me, saying, "Come, let us meet together in one of the villages in the plain of Ono." But they were planning to hurt or kill me. ³So I sent men with word to them, saying, "I am doing a great work and I cannot come down. Why should the work stop while I leave it and come

down to you?" 4They sent word to me four times in this way, and I gave them the same answer. . . .

15So the wall was finished . . . in fifty-two days. 16When all those who hated us heard about it, all the nations around us were afraid and troubled. For they saw that this work had been done with the help of our God. . . .

8:1Then all the people gathered . . . at the open space in front of the Water Gate. They asked Ezra the writer to bring the book of the Law of Moses which the Lord had given to Israel. . . . 3He read from it . . . from early morning until noon. He read it in front of men and women and those who were able to understand and all the people listened to the book of the Law. 4Ezra the writer stood on a raised floor of wood which they had made for this reason. . . . 6Then Ezra gave honor and thanks to the Lord the great God. And all the people answered, "Let it be so!" while lifting up their hands. They bowed low with their faces to the ground and worshiped the Lord.

Kid-Builder Value
COOPERATION means you are willing to work with other people to accomplish a task. God has given us different gifts and abilities and instructs us to cooperate with each other to accomplish His work. Nehemiah organized the building of the wall and encouraged his workers to cooperate to complete the job despite opposition.

KID-BUILDER Questions

- Why did Nehemiah want to rebuild the wall around Jerusalem?

- What trouble did Nehemiah and the people face as they rebuilt the wall?

- Nehemiah kept going even when trouble came. Have you ever felt like giving up in the middle of a big task? What helped you keep going?

- Think about a time when you worked hard on a project with someone else. How did you feel about working with a partner? What problems did you experience?

KID-BUILDER Prayer

Lord, help me work well with others, even if we don't always agree. Help me listen to other people's ideas and seek Your help for the best solution.

In Jesus' name. Amen.

Memory Verse:
The plans of those who do their best lead only to having all they need, but all who are in a hurry come only to want.   Prov. 21:5

ESTHER

Queen Esther

Esther 1—8

In those days King Ahasuerus sat on the king's throne in the city of Susa. ³In the third year of his rule, he gave a special supper for all his princes and leaders. . . .

¹⁰On the seventh day the heart of the king was happy with wine. And he told . . . the seven servants who served King Ahasuerus, ¹¹to bring Queen Vashti to the king with her crown. He wanted to show her beauty to the people and the princes. . . . ¹²But Queen Vashti would not come when the king sent his servants to bring her. So the king became very angry. . . . ¹³Then the king spoke to the wise men who understood the times. . . . ¹⁵He asked them, "By the law, what is to be done with Queen Vashti, because she did not obey what King Ahasuerus sent the servants to tell her?" ¹⁶Then Memucan said in front of the king and the princes, "Queen Vashti has done wrong not only to the king, but to all the princes and all the people in the lands of King Ahasuerus. . . . Let

the king give the place of queen to another who is better than she. . . ." ²¹What was said pleased the king and the princes, and the king did as Memucan said. . . .

²:⁵Now in the city of Susa where the king lived there was a Jew whose name was Mordecai. . . . ⁷He had brought up Hadassah, that is Esther, the daughter of his father's brother. For she did not have a father or mother. The young lady was beautiful in body and face. . . .

So Esther was taken to the king's house. . . . ¹⁰Esther had not told who her people or her family were because Mordecai had told her to say nothing. . . .

Esther found favor in the eyes of all who saw her. . . . ¹⁷And the king loved Esther more than all the women. She found favor and kindness with him, . . . so that he set the queen's crown on her head and made her queen instead of Vashti. . . .

³:¹After these things King Ahasuerus raised Haman . . . to a more important duty. He was made to rule over all the princes who were with him. ²All the king's servants who were at the king's gate bowed down and gave honor to Haman, for the king had said that this should be done. But Mordecai did not bow down or give him honor. . . . ⁵When Haman saw that Mordecai did not bow down or honor him, he was very angry. ⁶But he did not want to only hurt Mordecai. . . . He wanted to

destroy all the people of Mordecai in the whole nation of Ahasuerus. . . .

During this time, Mordecai found out about a plot to kill the king. He told Esther about it. Esther told the king. Meanwhile, Haman went to the king and requested that he write a letter stating that the

Jewish people were to be killed. Their lands could also be taken. Haman gave money to the king to make sure the Jewish people would be killed. Once this law was written, it could not be changed.

4:3There was much sorrow among the Jews in each and every part of the nation where the king's law was made known. . . .

4Then Esther's women and men servants came and told her, and the queen was very troubled. . . . 5Then Esther called Hathach from the king's servants. . . . She told him to go to Mordecai and find out what was wrong and why. . . . 7And Mordecai told him all that had happened. . . . And he said that she should go in to the king and beg him to show favor to her people. . . .

10Then Esther told Hathach to say to Mordecai, 11"All the king's servants and the people of the king's nation know that he has one law for any man or woman who comes to him in his room who has not been called: They will be put to death, unless the king holds out his special golden stick to him so that he may live. And I have not been called to come to the king for these thirty days.". . .

13Mordecai answered, "Do not think that you in the king's special house will live any more than all

Kid-Builder Fact
Josh. 7:21 *Shinar* is Hebrew for Babylonia.
Josh. 7:26 *Achor* means troubling.

the other Jews. 14For if you keep quiet at this time, help will come to the Jews from another place. But you and your father's house will be destroyed. Who knows if you have not become queen for such a time as this?" 15Then Esther told them to say to Mordecai, 16"Go, gather together all the Jews who are in Susa, and have them all go without food so they can pray better for me. . . . I and my women servants will go without food in the same way. Then I will go in to the king, which is against the law. And if I die, I die." 17So Mordecai went away and did just as Esther had told him.

5:1On the third day Esther put on her queen's clothing and stood in the open space inside the king's special house in front of his throne room. The king was sitting on his throne in the throne room looking toward the door of his house. 2When the king saw Esther, . . . she found favor in his eyes. The king held his special golden stick in his hand toward Esther. . . . 3Then the king said to her, "What do you want, Queen Esther? What do you ask of me? You would be given even as much as half the nation." 4Esther said, "If it please the king, may the king and Haman come today to the special supper I have made ready for him."

Haman and the king went to Esther's dinner party. She asked them to come to another party. Haman still hated Mordecai. He had a tower built where Mordecai would be killed. Meanwhile, the king remembered that Mordecai had saved his life. He wanted to honor Mordecai and asked for Haman's advice. Because Mordecai had favor with the king, Haman could not have him killed.

7:1So the king and Haman came to eat with Esther the queen. 2And the king said again to Esther . . . "What do you want to ask of me, Queen Esther? It will be done for you. . . ." 3Queen Esther answered, "If I have found favor in your eyes, O king, and if it please the king, I ask that my life and the lives of my people be saved. 4For I and my people have been sold, to be destroyed, to be killed, and to be done away with. . . ." 5Then King Ahasuerus asked Queen Esther, "Who is he, and where is he, who would do such a thing?" 6Esther said, "This sinful Haman hates us very much!" . . .

10So they hanged Haman on the tower that he had made for Mordecai. Then the king's anger became less.

8:1On that day King Ahasuerus gave everything Haman owned, the one who hated the Jews, to Queen Esther. . . . And Esther put Mordecai over everything Haman had owned.

3Then Esther spoke again to the king. She fell at his feet and cried and begged him to stop the sinful plan of Haman. . . . 4The king held out the special golden stick toward Esther. . . . 5Then she said, "If it pleases the king and if I have his favor . . . let letters be written to keep Haman's letters from being carried out. . . ."

¹¹In the letters the king allowed the Jews who were in every city the right to gather together to fight for their lives. He gave them the right to destroy, kill, and do away with the whole army of any people or nation which might come to fight against them. . . . And the letter was made known in the city of Susa where the king ruled. . . .

¹⁷In every part of the nation and in every city where the king's law had come, there was happiness and joy for the Jews, a special supper and a good day. And many people who had come there from other countries became Jews because they were afraid of the Jews.

Kid-Builder Value

COURAGE is the ability and willingness to stand firm when confronted by danger, fear, or peer pressure. Esther showed courage when she went before the king. Tough times bring out courage or fear in all of us. It's up to us to decide whether we will make courageous or fearful choices. God helps us to be people of courage.

KID-BUILDER Questions

- What was Haman's plot?

- What did Mordecai want Esther to do? What did Esther do?

- Going before the king took courage. It could have meant death for Esther. What is the scariest thing you have faced? What do you usually do when you're afraid?

- Courage and responsibility go hand in hand. Feeling responsible for her people gave Esther courage. What decisions do you have to make that take courage?

KID-BUILDER Prayer

Lord, help me be courageous and not give in to fear. In Jesus' name. Amen.

Memory Verse:
For God did not give us a spirit of fear. He gave us a spirit of power and of love and of a good mind.   II Tim. 1:7

POETRY &
WISDOM

The Books of *Poetry and Wisdom* include Job, Psalms, Proverbs, Ecclesiastes, and the Song of Solomon. They give wise sayings and advice for living lives that please God.

Job

Job (JOBE) says important things about suffering. It shows us right and wrong ideas and feelings about suffering through the life of a man. Job realizes that his trust in God should not depend on circumstances. This book helps us understand that God is in control of all things, and He will only allow things to happen to us that will help us grow and know Him better.

Psalms

The Book of *Psalms* (SALMZ) was used as a hymnbook by the Jewish people when they returned from exile in Babylon and rebuilt the temple. King David wrote seventy-three psalms. Solomon wrote two. Asaph wrote twelve. The Korahites (temple musicians) wrote nine. Moses wrote one. The writers of the rest of the psalms are unknown. The main theme of the book is praise.

JOB

Job's Suffering

Job 1—42

There was a man in the land of Uz whose name was Job. That man was without blame. He was right and good, he feared God, and turned away from sin. ²Seven sons and three daughters were born to him. ³He had 7000 sheep, 3000 camels, 1000 oxen, 500 female donkeys, and many servants. He was the greatest of all the men of the east. . . .

⁶Now there was a day when the sons of God came to show themselves before the Lord. Satan came with them also. ⁷And the Lord said to Satan, "Where have you come from?" Satan . . . said, "From traveling around on the earth. . . ." ⁸The Lord said to Satan, "Have you thought about My servant Job? For there is no one like him on the earth. He is without blame, a man who is right and good. He honors God with fear and turns away from sin." ⁹Then Satan answered the Lord, "Does Job fear God for nothing? ¹⁰Have You not made a wall around him and his house and all that

he has, on every side? You have brought good to the work of his hands, and he has received more and more in the land. ¹¹But put out Your hand now and touch all that he has. And for sure he will curse You to Your face." ¹²Then the Lord said to Satan, "See, all that he has is in your power. Only do not put your hand on him." . . .

¹³[One] day . . . ¹⁴ a man came to Job with news, saying, "The oxen were pulling the plow and the donkeys were eating beside them. ¹⁵And the Sabeans came and took them. They also killed the servants with the sword. I alone have run away from them to tell you." ¹⁶While he was still speaking, another man came and said, "The fire of God fell from heaven and burned up the sheep and the servants. . . . I alone have gotten away to tell you." ¹⁷While he was still speaking, another came and said, "The Babylonians divided into three groups and came to fight. They took the camels and killed the servants with the sword. I alone have gotten away to tell you." ¹⁸While he was still speaking, another also came and said, "Your sons and daughters were eating and drinking wine in their oldest brother's house. ¹⁹And see, a strong wind came from the desert and hit the four corners of the house. It fell on the young people and they are

Kid-Builder Fact
Job 1:15 The Sabeans were Arabs.

dead. I alone have gotten away to tell you."

20Then Job stood up and tore his clothing and cut the hair from his head. And he fell to the ground and worshiped. 21He said, "Without clothing I was born from my mother, and without clothing I will return. The Lord gave and the Lord has taken away. Praise the name of the Lord." 22In all this Job did not sin or blame God. . . .

2:9Then his wife said to him, "Do you still hold on to your faith? Curse God and die!" 10But he said to her, "You speak as one of the foolish women would speak. Should we receive good from God and not receive trouble?" In all this Job did not sin with his lips. . . .

42:10The Lord returned to Job all the things that he had lost. . . . The Lord gave Job twice as much as he had before.

Kid-Builder Value
PERSEVERANCE is the ability to keep going even under pressure without becoming discouraged. Job persevered through trials and suffering. His patience is a lesson for all of us to follow when trials come our way.

KID-BUILDER Questions

- What happened to Job?

- What did Job's wife suggest? Would that have helped? Why or why not?

- What happened to Job at the end?

- Sometimes trouble comes into our lives and won't let go. What helps you keep going when trouble comes?

- Job admitted his need for God in the midst of his trouble. How does God help you keep on going?

KID-BUILDER Prayer

Lord, when trouble comes, help me not to give up.
In Jesus' name. Amen.

Memory Verse:
These tests have come to prove your faith and to show that it is good.   I Pet. 1:7a

• •

PSALMS

God Is a Shepherd

Psalm 23

David was once a shepherd. In this psalm, he compares how the Lord takes care of His people in the same way a shepherd cares for his sheep.

The Lord is my Shepherd. I will have everything I need. ²He lets me rest in fields of green grass. He leads me beside the quiet waters. ³He makes me strong again. He leads me in the way of living right with Himself which brings honor to His name. ⁴Yes, even if I walk through the valley of the shadow of death, I will not be afraid of anything, because You are with me. You have a walking stick with which to guide and one with which to help. These comfort me. ⁵You are making a

Kid-Builder Fact
Ps. 23:5 Shepherds poured oil on the heads of their sheep to keep away flies and other insects and parasites that would torment the sheep. This is an image of how God soothes His people.

table of food ready for me in front of those who hate me. You have poured oil on my head. I have everything I need. 6For sure, You will give me goodness and loving-kindness all the days of my life. Then I will live with You in Your house forever.

God Helps His People

Psalm 46

God is our safe place and our strength. He is always our help when we are in trouble. ²So we will not be afraid, even if the earth is shaken and the mountains fall into the center of the sea, ³and even if its waters go wild with storm and the mountains shake with its action.

⁴There is a river whose waters make glad the city of God, the holy place where the Most High lives. ⁵God is in the center of her. She will not be moved. God will help her when the morning comes. ⁶The people made noise. The nations fell. He raised His voice and the earth melted. ⁷The Lord of All is with us. The God of Jacob is our strong place.

⁸Come and see the works of the Lord. He has

Kid-Builder Fact
Ps. 46:1 The psalms often inspired our present-day hymns. Psalm 46 inspired Martin Luther to write the hymn "A Mighty Fortress Is Our God."

destroyed parts of the earth. ⁹He stops wars to the ends of the earth. He breaks the bow and cuts the spear in two. He burns the [chariots] with fire. ¹⁰Be quiet and know that I am God. I will be honored among the nations. I will be honored in the earth. ¹¹The Lord of All is with us. The God of Jacob is our strong place.

Kid-Builder Value
CONFIDENCE is a feeling of security based on faith and trust. God tells us through the psalms that we can trust Him. Through Him, we have everything we need.

• •

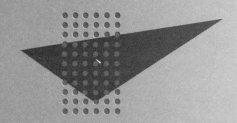

KID-BUILDER Questions

- In Psalm 23, how does God help His people?

- What hope does Psalm 46 express?

- Both psalms talk of how God helps His people. How can these psalms help you have confidence to seek God for help?

- Try writing a psalm of your own. What would you say about God?

KID-BUILDER Prayer

Lord, thank You for providing for my needs and for giving me the confidence to know that You are my help in times of trouble.   In Jesus' name. Amen.

Memory Verse:
The Lord is my Shepherd. I will have everything I need. Ps. 23:1

PSALMS

The Importance of God's Word

Psalm 119

Happy are those whose way is without blame, who walk in the Law of the Lord. 2Happy are those who keep His Law and look for Him with all their heart. . . .

9How can a young man keep his way pure? By living by Your Word. . . . 11Your Word have I hid in my heart, that I may not sin against You. . . .

33O Lord, teach me the way of Your Law and I will obey it to the end. 34Give me understanding. Then I will listen to Your Word and obey it with all my heart. 35Make me walk in the path of Your Word, for I find joy in it. 36Turn my heart toward Your Law, so I will not earn money in a wrong way. 37Turn my eyes away from things that have no worth, and give me new life because of Your ways. . . .

66Teach me what I should know to be right and fair for I believe in Your law. . . . 89Forever, O Lord, Your Word will never change in heaven. . . .

105Your Word is a lamp to my feet and a light to my path. . . .

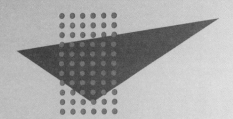

Psalm 119 is the longest chapter in the Bible. It has 176 verses. Many of those verses talk about God's Word. Though many different people wrote different parts of the Bible, they weren't writing down their own ideas and words. God gave them the words to use. The Bible contains what God wants everyone to know about Him and about how to obey Him.

The Bible teaches us about Jesus, God's Son. Because Jesus gave Himself as a sacrifice for our sin, we can be a part of God's family and live with Him someday in heaven. As we read His Word every day, God can show us the things in our lives that don't please Him. We can tell Him we are sorry for our sins and know that He forgives us.

The Bible also teaches us how to live. We can learn how to live the way God wants us to live by reading His Word. In doing so, we will please God and be happy, too. The important thing to remember is that we have to read God's Word to know what it says, and then follow what God says to do.

God's Word will last forever, even when the pages and cover are gone. It will always be true. It never changes.

Memorizing portions of the Bible lets us take God's Word with us wherever we go. Here is a list of Scriptures from your *Kid-Builder Bible* to get you started.

Psalm 23	John 14:1-3	I Corinthians 13
Genesis 1:1-3, 26	Exodus 20:1-17	John 3:3-6, 16

Memory Verse:
Your Word have I hid in my heart, that I may not sin against You.
Ps. 119:11

Proverbs

Proverbs (PRAH-vurbz) is a book of wise sayings. King Solomon, the wisest man in the world, wrote most of these sayings. This book, with its thirty-one chapters, can be considered a how-to book on how to become wise. The first step is to trust God.

Ecclesiastes

Ecclesiastes (ee-klee-zee-AS-teez) was probably also written by Solomon during his later years. He points out the wisdom of following God in contrast to worshiping things in place of God. Having tried everything, Solomon wound up seeing life as empty and meaningless apart from serving God.

Song of Solomon

Song of Solomon (Song of SAHL-uh-munn) is a love story. It tells about the love between King Solomon and his bride. It describes the feelings they have for each other. Many people also see in the book a picture of God's love for Israel, or Christ's love for the church.

PROVERBS

Words of Wisdom

Proverbs 1—29

These are the wise sayings of Solomon, son of David, king of Israel: ²They show you how to know wisdom and teaching, to find the words of understanding. ³They help you learn about the ways of wisdom and what is right and fair. . . . ⁷The fear of the Lord is the beginning of much learning. Fools hate wisdom and teaching. . . .

3:5Trust in the Lord with all your heart, and do not trust in your own understanding. ⁶Think of Him in all your ways, and He will make your paths straight. . . .

6:16There are six things which the Lord hates, yes, seven that are hated by Him: ¹⁷A proud look, a lying tongue, and hands that kill those who are without guilt, ¹⁸a heart that makes sinful plans, feet that run fast to sin, ¹⁹a person who tells lies about someone else, and one who starts fights among brothers. . . .

11:13He who is always telling stories makes secrets known, but he who can be trusted keeps a thing hidden. . . .

11:17The man who shows loving-kindness does himself good, but the man without pity hurts himself. . . . 20The Lord hates those who are sinful in heart, but those who walk without blame are His joy. . . .25The man who gives much will have much, and he who helps others will be helped himself. . . .

12:17He who speaks the truth tells what is right, but a liar tells lies. . . .

13:1A wise son listens when his father tells him the right way, but one who laughs at the truth does not listen when strong words are spoken to him. . . . 16Every wise man acts with much learning, but a fool makes his foolish way known. . . .

14:29He who is slow to get angry has great understanding, but he who has a quick temper makes his foolish way look right. . . .

15:1A gentle answer turns away anger, but a sharp word causes anger. . . .

16:18Pride comes before being destroyed and a proud spirit comes before a fall. 19It is better to be

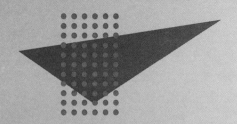

KID-BUILDER Questions

- How would you explain in your own words the phrase "He has made everything beautiful in its time"?

- How can knowing that God is in control of the times of your life give you comfort? How could you share this with a friend?

- How does God teach us patience in difficult circumstances? Do you think that God could teach us to be patient any other way? Why or why not?

KID-BUILDER Prayer

Lord, when things seem out of control, help me remember that You are still in control and You are working everything out for my good.

In Jesus' name. Amen.

Memory Verse:
There is a special time for everything. There is a time for everything that happens under heaven.   Eccl. 3:1

THE PROPHETS

The Books of *The Prophets* are Isaiah through the Book of Malachi. These books give direct messages from God through men called prophets. There are two categories of *prophets*—major and minor. The books of the major prophets are: Isaiah, Jeremiah, Lamentations, Ezekiel, and Daniel. The minor prophets are Hosea, Joel, Amos, Obadiah, Jonah, Micah, Nahum, Habakkuk, Zephaniah, Haggai, Zachariah, and Malachi.

The Major Prophets

Isaiah

The Book of *Isaiah* (eye-ZAY-ah) is quoted more times in the New Testament than all the other prophets combined. Isaiah looked for the coming of the Messiah. The book was written to warn the nation of Israel that a righteous God must punish sin. Isaiah warned them to stop their wicked habits and ask God for His forgiveness.

Jeremiah

Jeremiah (JER-uh-MY-uh) is the longest prophetic book in the Old Testament. It was written by the prophet Jeremiah, who also wrote the Book of Lamentations. This book describes events that happened in Jeremiah's life and in the history of the southern kingdom of Judah between 625 and 580 B.C.

Lamentations

Lamentations (LAM-en-TAY-shuns) is a book of tears. Jeremiah writes this book after the destruction of Jerusalem when many people are hungry and suffering because their families have been taken away to Babylon. The prophet Jeremiah suffers with them, but he is still able to write about the faithfulness of God.

Ezekiel

Ezekiel (ee-ZEE-kee-ul) is one of the important prophetic books of the Old Testament. It is written by Ezekiel, a Jewish prophet who lives in exile in Babylon with other people of Judah. Ezekiel teaches the people that God is with them in Babylon just as much as He had been with them in Judah. He encourages the people to obey God wherever they are.

Daniel

Daniel (DAN-yull) is best known for being thrown into a den of lions when he refused to stop worshiping God. His book was written during the time of Israel's exile. Because of Israel's sin, God allowed them to be conquered and captured by the Assyrians and Babylonians. Many of the Israelites, including Daniel, were taken away to live in Babylon. The righteousness of Daniel and his three friends—Shadrach, Meshach, and Abednego—was often put to the test.

DANIEL

The Fiery Furnace

Daniel 3

King Nebuchadnezzar made an object of gold. . . . It was fifteen times taller than a man, and as wide as three long steps. He set it up . . . in the land of Babylon. ²Then Nebuchadnezzar called together all the captains, leaders, rulers, wise men, money-keepers, judges, and law-keepers of Babylon's lands. . . . ⁴Then the man who spread news for the king said in a loud voice, "This is what you must do, O people . . . ⁵When you hear the sound of the horns and [harps], and all kinds of music, you are to . . . worship the object of gold that King Nebuchadnezzar has set up. ⁶Whoever does not . . . worship will be thrown at once into the . . . fire." ⁷Then all the people heard the sound of the horns and [harps]. . . . All the people . . . worshiped the object of gold. . . .

⁸At this time certain ones who learned from stars came up and spoke against the Jews. ⁹They said to King Nebuchadnezzar, "O king, live forever! ¹⁰You yourself, O king, have made a law that every

man who hears the sound of the horns and [harps] and all kinds of music is to get down on his knees and worship the object of gold. [11]And whoever does not . . . worship must be thrown into the . . . fire. [12]There are certain Jews whom you have chosen as leaders over the land of Babylon. Their names are Shadrach, Meshach, and Abed-nego. These men . . . do not serve your gods or worship the object of gold which you have set up."

[13]Then Nebuchadnezzar became very angry and called for Shadrach, Meshach, and Abed-nego. And they were brought to the king.

[14]Nebuchadnezzar said to them, "Is it true, Shadrach, Meshach and Abed-nego, that you do not serve my gods or worship the object of gold that I have set up? [15]Now if you are ready to get down on your knees and worship the object I have made when you hear the sound of the horns and [harps] . . . , very well. But if you will not worship, you will be thrown at once into the fire. And what god is able to save you from my hands?"

[16]Shadrach, Meshach and Abed-nego answered and said to the king, "O Nebuchadnezzar, we do not need to give you an answer to this question. [17]If we are thrown into the fire, our God Whom we serve is able to save us from it. And He will save us from your hand, O king. [18]But even if He does not, we want you to know, O king, that we will not serve your gods or wor-

ship the object of gold that you have set up."

¹⁹Then Nebuchadnezzar was filled with anger. . . . He had the fire made seven times hotter. . . . ²⁰And he told certain powerful soldiers in his army to tie up Shadrach, Meshach and Abednego, and to throw them into the fire. . . . ²²Because the king had spoken that the fire was to be very hot, those men who put Shadrach, Meshach and Abed-nego into the fire were killed by the fire. ²³The three men were still tied up when they fell into the fire.

²⁴Then King Nebuchadnezzar . . . said to his leaders, "Did we not throw three men . . . into the fire?" They answered, "That is true, O king." ²⁵He said, "Look! I see four men loose and walking about in the fire without being hurt! And the

fourth one looks like . . . (the Son of God)!"

²⁶Then Nebuchadnezzar came near the door where the fire was burning, and said, "Shadrach, Meshach and Abed-nego, servants of the Most High God, come out! . . ." So Shadrach, Meshach and Abed-nego came out of the fire. ²⁷The . . . king's important men . . . saw that the fire had not hurt the bodies of these three men. Their hair was not burned. Their clothes were not burned. They did not even smell like fire.

²⁸Nebuchadnezzar said, "Praise be to the God of Shadrach, Meshach, and Abed-nego. He has sent His angel and saved His servants who put their trust in Him. They . . . were ready to give up their lives instead of . . . worshiping any god except their own God. ²⁹So I now make a law that if any people of any nation or language say anything against the God of Shadrach, Meshach and Abed-nego, they will be torn apart and their houses will be laid waste. For there is no other god who is able to save in this way." ³⁰Then the king made Shadrach, Meshach and Abed-nego very important in the land of Babylon.

Kid-Builder Value
CONVICTION is a strong belief in a moral standard. Your convictions are the things you hold to be right or wrong. They mold your thoughts and actions. Shadrach, Meshach, and Abed-nego had conviction to obey God, even though they were threatened with death.

KID-BUILDER Questions

- What was the king's law? How did Shadrach, Meshach, and Abed-nego respond?

- How did God help them?

- Have you ever had to stand up for your beliefs? What happened? Would you do it again? Why or why not?

- Many Christians through the ages have been persecuted for their beliefs. If there was the slightest chance of that happening to you, what would you do?

KID-BUILDER Prayer

Lord, I want to believe in You, even through times of trouble. But I need Your help. Help me do what is right.   *In Jesus' name. Amen.*

Memory Verse:
The Good News did not come to you by word only, but with power and through the Holy Spirit. You knew it was true.   I Thess. 1:5a

DANIEL

Daniel in the Lions' Den

Daniel 6

At this time, Daniel is about eighty years old. He had lived through the reign of King Nebuchadnezzar. Now the Medes and the Persians have taken over. Darius is on the throne.

It pleased Darius to choose 120 captains to rule over the people. They would rule over the whole nation. ²And three leaders were to rule over them, and Daniel was one. . . . ³Then Daniel showed that he could do better work than the other leaders and captains because a special spirit was in him. So the king planned to give him power over the whole nation. ⁴Then the leaders and captains tried to find a reason to complain against Daniel. . . . But they could not find . . . anything to blame him for, because he was faithful and honest and did not do anything wrong. ⁵Then these men said, "We will not find anything to say against Daniel unless it has to do with the Law of his God."

³So these leaders and captains came as a group to the king and said, "King Darius, live forever! ⁷All

the leaders of the nation . . . have spoken with each other and have agreed that a new law should be made. The king should make a law . . . saying that anyone who asks something of any god or man besides you, O king, for thirty days, must be thrown to the lions. . . . 8It will be by the law of the Medes and Persians, and cannot be changed." 9So King Darius made the law and wrote his name on it.

10When Daniel knew that the king had written his name on this law, he went into his house where, in his upper room, he had windows open toward Jerusalem. There he got down on his knees three times each day, praying and giving thanks to his God, as he had done before. 11Then these men . . . found Daniel praying. . . . 12So they went to the king . . . saying, "Did you not write your name on a law which says that anyone who asks something of any god or man besides you, O king, for thirty days, is to be thrown to the lions?" The king answered, "This is true. It is by the law of the Medes and Persians, which cannot be changed." 13Then they said to the king, "Daniel . . . is still asking things of his God three times a day." 14When the king heard this, he was very troubled and tried to think of a way to save Daniel. Even until sunset he was trying to find a way to save him. 15Then these men . . . said, "Understand, O king, that it is a law of the Medes and Persians that any law the

king makes cannot be changed."

16So the king had Daniel brought in and thrown into the place where lions were kept. The king said to Daniel, "May your God, Whom you are faithful to serve, save you." 17And a stone was brought and laid over the mouth of the hole. The king marked it with his own special ring and with the rings of his important men, so that no one could save Daniel. 18Then the king went to his beautiful house and spent the night without food and sleep. And nothing was brought to make him feel better.

19The king got up at sunrise and went in a hurry to the place where lions were kept. 20When he came to the hole in the ground where Daniel was, he called to him with a troubled voice, "Daniel, servant of the living God, has your God, Whom you always serve, been able to save you from the lions?" 21Then Daniel said to the king, "O king, live forever! 22My God sent His angel and shut the lions' mouths. They have not hurt me, because He knows that . . . I have done nothing wrong to you, O king." 23Then the king was very pleased and had Daniel taken up out of the hole in the ground. So they took Daniel out of the hole and saw that he had not been hurt at all, because he had trusted in

Kid-Builder Fact
Dan. 6:16 The den of lions was probably a deep pit in the ground with an opening at the top. Daniel had to be lowered into the den.

his God. 24Then the king had those men brought to him who had spoken against Daniel. And they threw them with their wives and children into the hole with the lions. Even before they hit the

bottom of the hole, the lions went after them and crushed all their bones.

25Then King Darius wrote to all the people of every nation. . . . He wrote, "May you have much peace! 26I make a law that all those under my rule are to fear . . . the God of Daniel. For He is the living God and He lives forever. . . . 27He saves and brings men out of danger, and shows His great power in heaven and on earth. And He has saved Daniel from the power of the lions."

28So things went well for Daniel during the rule of Darius and during the rule of Cyrus the Persian.

Kid-Builder Value
CONFIDENCE is a feeling of security based on faith and trust. Daniel had confidence in God, even though he was thrown into a den of lions. Confidence isn't based on circumstances. It is based on one's relationship with God.

KID-BUILDER Questions

- What was the law? How did Daniel break the law?

- What was Daniel's punishment? How did God come through for him?

- Have you ever been punished for doing the right thing? What happened?

- How confident do you feel about God's ability to help you? Does confidence depend on feelings?

KID-BUILDER Prayer

Lord, help me place my confidence in You.
In Jesus' name. Amen.

Memory Verse:
My heart will not be moved, O God. My heart cannot be moved. I will sing, yes, I will sing praises!   Ps. 57:7

THE PROPHETS

The Minor Prophets

Hosea, Joel, Amos, Obadiah, Jonah, Micah, Nahum, Habakkuk, Zephaniah, Haggai, Zechariah, Malachi

The last twelve books of the Old Testament are called *The Minor Prophets*. We call them "minor" because they are shorter than the five "major" prophetic books.

Even though these prophets lived during a time of destruction and captivity, God enabled them to look ahead to some exciting things that God had planned. One of the greatest of these promises was the birth of a Savior, Jesus Christ, who would one day be born in Bethlehem.

Each of the *Minor Prophets* has a central message:

Hosea (hoe-ZAY-uh)—God's love and forgiveness
Joel (JO-el)—God punishes and restores
Amos (AY-mus)—Taking responsibility for life choices
Obadiah (OH-buh-DIE-uh)—God will rule the earth
Jonah (JO-nuh)—A prophet learns to obey
Micah (MY-cuh)—God has a plan for the world
Nahum (NAY-hum)—God's strength and power
Habakkuk (huh-BACK-uk)—Learning to trust God
Zephaniah (zef-uh-NY-uh)—God will judge the world
Haggai (HAG-ee-eye)—Rebuilding the temple
Zechariah (ZEK-uh-RYE-uh)—Visions of a coming king
Malachi (MAL-uh-kie)—Promised blessing and hope

JONAH

Jonah

Jonah 1—4

The word of the Lord came to Jonah the son of Amittai, saying, ²"Get up and go to the large city of Nineveh, and preach against it. For their sin has come up before Me." ³But Jonah ran away from the Lord going toward Tarshish. He went down to Joppa and found a ship which was going to Tarshish. . . .

⁴Then the Lord sent a powerful wind upon the sea, and there was such a big storm that the ship was about to break up. ⁵The sailors became afraid, and every man cried to his god. They threw the things that were in the ship into the sea so that it would not be so heavy. But Jonah had gone below in the ship and . . . fallen asleep. ⁶So the captain went to him and said, "How can you sleep? Get up and call on your god. It may be that your god will care about us, and we will not die." ⁷Then the sailors said to each other, "Come, let us draw names so we can find out who is to blame for this trouble." So they drew names, and Jonah's name

was drawn. ⁸Then they said to him, "Now tell us! Who is to blame for this? What is your work? Where do you come from?". . . ⁹Jonah said to them, "I am a Hebrew, and I worship the Lord God of heaven Who made the sea and the dry land."

¹⁰Then the men were filled with fear. . . . ¹¹So they said to him, "What should we do to you to make the sea quiet down for

us?" For the storm was getting worse.

¹²Jonah said to them, "Pick me up and throw me into the sea. Then the sea will quiet down for you. For I know that this bad storm has come upon you because of me." ¹³The men rowed hard to return to land, but they could not, for the wind was blowing even worse against them. ¹⁴Then they called on the Lord and said, "We beg You, O Lord, do not let us die for what this man has done. And do not let us become guilty for killing someone who is not to blame. . . ."

¹⁵So they picked up Jonah and threw him into the sea, and the storm stopped. ¹⁶Then the men feared the Lord very much. They gave a gift in worship to the Lord. . . .

¹⁷The Lord sent a big fish to swallow Jonah, and he was in the stomach of the fish for three days and three nights.

²:¹Then Jonah prayed to the Lord his God while in the stomach of the fish, ²saying, "I called out of my trouble to the Lord, and He answered me. I cried for help from the place of the dead, and You heard my voice. . . ."

¹⁰Then the Lord spoke to the fish, and it spit Jonah out onto the dry land.

³:¹The word of the Lord came to Jonah a second time, saying, ²"Get up and go to the large city of Nineveh, and tell the people there the news which I am going to tell you." ³So Jonah got up and went

to Nineveh, as the Lord had told him. Now Nineveh was a very large city. It took three days to walk through it. ⁴Jonah started into the city, for a day's walk, and he cried out, "In forty days Nineveh will be destroyed!"

⁵Then the people of Nineveh believed in God. They called for a time when no food was to be eaten. And all the people, from the greatest to the least, put on clothes made from hair. ⁶When the news came to the king of Nineveh, he got up from his throne and laid aside his beautiful clothing. Then he covered himself with cloth made from hair, and sat in ashes. ⁷And he sent word through all of Nineveh, saying, ". . . ⁸Everyone must pray to God with all his heart, so each person may turn from his sinful way and from the bad things he has done. ⁹Who knows? God may change His mind and stop being angry so that we will not die."

¹⁰When God saw what they did, and that they turned from their sinful way, He changed His mind about the trouble He said He would bring upon them, and He did not destroy Nineveh.

Kid-Builder Value
OBEDIENCE is doing what you're instructed to do.
Jonah failed to obey God and suffered the consequences.

KID-BUILDER Questions

- Where did God want Jonah to go? Where did he go instead?

- How did God get Jonah to be obedient?

- No one gets away with disobedience for long! Have you ever faced punishment after you thought you could get away with something wrong? What happened?

- What are some of the things your parents or teachers might have wanted you to do that you didn't want to do? Why do you think they wanted you to be obedient?

KID-BUILDER Prayer

Lord, help me be obedient, even when I want to follow my own way.　　　　　*In Jesus' name. Amen.*

Memory Verse:
Whoever obeys His Word has the love of God made perfect in him. This is the way to know if you belong to Christ.　　　I John 2:5

The New Testament

The *New Testament* has twenty-seven books. It covers God's New Covenant or "agreement" with people. Under the new agreement, we can come directly to Jesus for our salvation, and He has promised us a home with Him forever in heaven if we believe in Him.

As with the Old Testament, books in the *New Testament* are divided into sections. The first four books are called the *Gospels*. They tell us about Jesus Christ—how He lived, what He did, and how He died and rose again. *Church History* is the second section and it has only one book—the Acts of the Apostles. It tells us how the New Testament church began and how it grew. The books of the third section (the *Letters*) are actual letters written by the apostle Paul and others to help the people in specific churches follow Jesus and obey His Word. Finally, the book of *Prophecy* or Revelation tells us the secrets that God shared with John about the things that are yet to come.

The Gospels

The Gospels were written at different times during the first century. The books of Matthew, Mark, and Luke sound a lot alike in the events they include. Each Gospel writer had one main group of people he wanted to reach. Matthew and John wrote to the Jews. Mark and Luke wrote to those who were not Jews (Gentiles). All were concerned about presenting the life of Christ.

Around 150 A.D., the four books were combined into one Gospel, with each writer having a section. That way, the information in each book could be compared. Different people remembered different things and told what they knew about Jesus. Finally, all of these were put together in one book (the New Testament) so we have a full picture of the life of Christ.

Not all of the Gospels have the same stories. Sometimes this may seem confusing, so we have given you a list of the events of Jesus' life in the order they occurred. We have indicated with an *X* where each story is found in your *Kid-Builder Bible*.

Life of Jesus Outline

	Matthew	Mark	Luke	John
Birth Announcements			X	
Angel Appears to Joseph	X			
Jesus Is Born	X		X	
Visit by Shepherds			X	
The Wise Men Find Jesus	X			
Jesus Talks to Temple Leaders			X	
Jesus Is Baptized	X			
Miracle at a Wedding				X
Nicodemus Asks Jesus about Life				X
Jesus Calls Disciples to Follow Him				X
Jesus Teaches on the Mountain	X			
The Lord's Prayer	X			
An Army Captain Shows Faith in Jesus	X			
Jesus Heals a Paralyzed Man		X		
Jesus Calms the Storm			X	
Jairus's Daughter		X		
Jesus Feeds Five Thousand				X
Jesus Heals a Man Born Blind				X
The Good Samaritan			X	
The Prodigal Son			X	
Ten Lepers			X	
Jesus Brings Lazarus Back to Life				X
Triumphal Entry		X		
The Last Supper				X
Jesus' Arrest and Crucifixion	X			
Peter's Denial		X		
Jesus Is Raised from the Grave				X
Jesus Appears to His Followers				X

MATTHEW

Matthew was a former tax collector and a follower of Jesus. He wanted Jews to know that the Messiah had come.

An Angel Appears to Joseph

Matthew 1

The birth of Jesus Christ was like this: Mary His mother had been promised in marriage to Joseph. Before they were married, it was learned that she was to have a baby by the Holy Spirit. [19]Joseph . . . was a good man and did not want to make it hard for Mary in front of people. He thought it would be good to break the promised marriage without people knowing it. [20]While he was thinking about this, an angel of the Lord came to him in a dream. The angel said, "Joseph, son of David, do not be afraid to take Mary as your wife.

Kid-Builder Value
OBEDIENCE is doing what you're instructed to do. Joseph was obedient when he was told to take Mary as his wife, even though he was not sure he should marry her.

She is to become a mother by the Holy Spirit. 21A Son will be born to her. You will give Him the name Jesus because He will save His people from the punishment of their sins."

22This happened as the Lord said it would happen through the early preacher. 23He said, "The young woman, who has never had a man, will give birth to a Son. They will give Him the name Immanuel. This means God with us." (Isa. 7:14)

24Joseph awoke from his sleep. He did what the angel of the Lord told him to do. He took Mary as his wife. 25But he did not have her, as a husband has a wife, until she gave birth to a Son. Joseph gave Him the name Jesus.

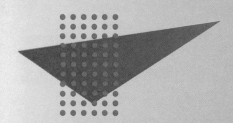

KID-BUILDER Questions

- What did Joseph want to do when he learned Mary was pregnant?

- Joseph wanted to do the right thing for Mary. He was also willing to obey God. On a scale of 1 to 10 (one being least willing), rate your own willingness to obey in these situations:
    - If obeying God means losing a friend
    - If obeying God means looking foolish in front of someone else

KID-BUILDER Prayer

Lord, sometimes being obedient means swallowing my pride to obey Your commands. Teach me how to obey You more seriously.

In Jesus' name. Amen.

Memory Verse:
I will show you and teach you in the way you should go. I will tell you what to do with My eye upon you.   Ps. 32:8

MATTHEW

The Wise Men Find Jesus

Matthew 2

Jesus was born in the town of Bethlehem in the country of Judea. It was the time when Herod was king of that part of the country. Soon after Jesus was born, some wise men who learned things from stars came to Jerusalem from the East. 2They asked, "Where is the King of the Jews Who has been born? We have seen His star in the East. We have come to worship Him."

3King Herod heard this. He and all the people of Jerusalem were worried. 4He called together all the religious leaders of the Jews and the teachers of the Law. Herod asked them where Christ was to be born. 5They said to him, "In Bethlehem of Judea...."

7Then Herod had a secret meeting with the men who learned things from stars. He asked them about what time the star had been seen. 8He sent them to Bethlehem and said, "Go and find the young Child. When you find Him, let me know. Then I can go and worship Him also."

9After the king had spoken, they went on their way. The star they had seen in the East went before them. It came and stopped over the place where the young Child was. 10When they saw the star, they were filled with much joy.

11They went into the house and found the young Child with Mary, His mother. Then they got down before Him and worshiped Him. They opened their bags of riches and gave Him gifts of gold and perfume and spices. 12Then God spoke to them in a dream. He told them not to go back to Herod. So they went to their own country by another road.

13When they had gone, an angel of the Lord came to Joseph in a dream. He said, "Get up. Take the young Child and His mother to the country of Egypt. Go as fast as you can! Stay there until you hear from Me. Herod is going to look for the young Child to kill Him." 14During the night he got up and left with the young Child and His mother for Egypt. 15He stayed there until Herod died. This happened as the Lord had said through an early preacher, "I called My Son out of Egypt."(Hos. 11:1)

16Herod learned that the wise men had fooled him. He was very angry. He sent men to kill all the young boys two years old and under in Bethlehem

Kid-Builder Value
COMMITMENT is a willingness to serve someone or a cause. The wise men showed commitment in their search for Jesus.

and in all the country near by. He decided to do this from what he had heard from the wise men as to the time when the star was seen. . . .

¹⁹After Herod died, an angel of the Lord came to Joseph in a dream while he was in Egypt. ²⁰He said, "Get up. Take the young Child and His mother and go into the land of the Jews. Those who tried to kill the young Child are dead." ²¹Joseph got up. He took the young Child and His mother and came into the land of the Jews. . . . God told him in a dream to go to the country of Galilee and he went. ²³Joseph stayed in a town called Nazareth. It happened as the early preachers said it would happen. They said, "Jesus will be called a Nazarene."

KID-BUILDER Questions

- Why did Herod want Jesus to be found?

- How did God protect Jesus?

- What plans or goals do you have for the future? Do you know what you want to be? what college you'd like to go to someday? How committed are you to those plans?

KID-BUILDER Prayer

Lord, help me be committed to You and to the tasks I have to do.   *In Jesus' name. Amen.*

Memory Verse:
Think of [God] in all your ways, and He will make your paths straight.   Prov. 3:6

Jesus Is Baptized

Matthew 3

In those days John the Baptist came preaching in the desert in the country of Judea. ²He said, "Be sorry for your sins and turn from them! The holy nation of heaven is near." ³The early preacher Isaiah spoke of this man. He said, "Listen! His voice calls out in the desert! 'Make the way ready for the Lord. Make the road straight for Him!'" (Isa. 40:3)

⁴John wore clothes made of hair from camels. He had a leather belt around him. His food was locusts and wild honey.

⁵Then the people of Jerusalem and of all the country of Judea and those from near the Jordan

Kid-Builder Fact
Matt. 3:13 In Moses' day, baptism simply meant washing (Exod. 30:17-21). But when John the Baptist called the crowds to be baptized, he was asking them to be washed inside and outside (Matt. 3:1-6). The outside washing showed that the person wanted to be changed on the inside. Baptism meant a person was asking God to forgive his or her sins.

River went to him. 6Those who told of their sins were baptized by him in the Jordan River. 7He saw many proud religious law-keepers and other people of the religious group who believe no one will be raised from the dead. They were coming to him to be baptized. He said to them, "You family of snakes! Who told you how to keep from God's anger that is coming? 8Do something to show me that your hearts are changed. . . . 11For sure, I baptize with water those who are sorry for their sins and turn from them. The One Who comes after me will baptize you with the Holy Spirit and with fire. He is greater than I. I am not good enough to take off His shoes. 12He comes ready to clean the grain. He will gather the grain in and clean it all. The clean grain He will put into a building. He will burn that which is no good with a fire that cannot be put out."

13Jesus came from Galilee. He went to John at the Jordan River to be baptized by him. 14John tried to stop Him. He said, "I need to be baptized by You. Do You come to me?" 15Jesus said to him, "Let it be done now. We should do what is right." John agreed and baptized Jesus. 16When Jesus came up out of the water, the heavens opened. He saw the Spirit of God coming down and resting on Jesus like a dove. 17A voice was heard from heaven. It said, "This is My much-loved Son. I am very happy with Him."

Kid-Builder Value
REPENTANCE is sorrow for one's sin, and turning away from that sin to serve God and do right. John the Baptist preached the importance of repentance.

KID-BUILDER Questions

- Jesus was baptized too, but not because He needed to repent. He wanted to show His commitment to the work ahead. His commitment makes repentance possible. What does repentance mean to you?

- Have you wanted to repent but aren't sure how to go about doing that? You can pray the prayer below.

KID-BUILDER Prayer

Lord, I'm sorry for the things I've done wrong. Please forgive me and cleanse me. I am committed to tell others about You.   *In Jesus' name. Amen.*

Memory Verse:
Be sorry for your sins and turn from them! The holy nation of heaven is near.

Matt. 3:2

MATTHEW

Jesus taught us many ways to please God and build friendships with others in the Sermon on the Mount.

Jesus Teaches on the Mountain

Matthew 5—7

Jesus . . . went up on the mountain and sat down. His followers came to Him. ²He began to teach them, saying, ³"Those who know there is nothing good in themselves are happy, because the holy nation of heaven is theirs. ⁴Those who have sorrow are happy, because they will be comforted. ⁵Those who have no pride in their hearts are happy, because the earth will be given to them. ⁶Those who are hungry and thirsty to be right with God are happy, because they will be filled. ⁷Those who show loving-kindness are happy, because they will have loving-kindness shown to them. ⁸Those who have a pure heart are happy, because they will see God. ⁹Those who make peace are happy, because they will be called the sons of God. ¹⁰Those who have it very hard for doing right are happy, because the holy nation of heaven is theirs. ¹¹You are happy when people act and talk in a bad way to

you and make it very hard for you ... because you
trust in Me. [12]Be glad and full of joy because your
pay will be much in heaven. . . .

[38]"You have heard that it has been said, 'An eye
for an eye and a tooth for a tooth.' [39]But I tell you,
do not fight with the man who wants to fight.

Whoever hits you on the right side of the face, turn so he can hit the other side also. 40If any person takes you to court to get your shirt, give him your coat also. 41Whoever makes you walk a short way, go with him twice as far. 42Give to any person who asks you for something. Do not say no to the man who wants to use something of yours.

43"You have heard that it has been said, 'You must love your neighbor and hate those who hate you.' 44But I tell you, love those who hate you. (Respect and give thanks for those who say bad things to you. Do good to those who hate you.) Pray for those who do bad things to you and who make it hard for you. . . .

7:12"Do for other people whatever you would like to have them do for you. . . ."

Kid-Builder Value
FRIENDLINESS is a mutual feeling of affection between two people. In the Sermon on the Mount, Jesus gave us rules to follow to develop friendships. He told us that we must love those who are against us, be merciful and forgiving, be peace-makers, and pray for those who do bad things to us.

KID-BUILDER Questions

• Do you consider yourself a happy person? Why? What kinds of people did Jesus say are happy (or blessed)? Are those reasons the same or different from the reasons you gave for being happy?

• How do we show others by our actions that we are Christians?

KID-BUILDER Prayer

Lord, help me to please You in my friendships with others. Show me how I can be more like You in my attitudes and actions. *In Jesus' name. Amen.*

Memory Verse:
Let your light shine in front of men. Then they will see the good things you do and will honor your Father Who is in heaven.

Matt. 5:16

The Lord's Prayer

Matthew 6

When you pray, do not say the same thing over and over again making long prayers like the people who do not know God. They think they are heard because their prayers are long. 8Do not be like them. Your Father knows what you need before you ask Him.

9"Pray like this: 'Our Father in heaven, Your name is holy. 10May Your holy nation come. What You want done, may it be done on earth as it is in heaven. 11Give us the bread we need today. 12Forgive us our sins as we forgive those who sin against us.

13" 'Do not let us be tempted, but keep us from sin. Your nation is holy. You have power and shining greatness forever. Let it be so.'

14"If you forgive people their sins, your Father in heaven will forgive your sins also. 15If you do not forgive people their sins, your Father will not forgive your sins. . . .

7:7"Ask, and what you are asking for will be given

to you. Look, and what you are looking for you will find. Knock, and the door you are knocking on will be opened to you. ⁸Everyone who asks receives what he asks for. Everyone who looks finds what he is looking for. Everyone who knocks has the door opened to him. ⁹What man among you would give his son a stone if he should ask for bread? ¹⁰Or if he asks for a fish, would he give him a snake? ¹¹You are bad and you know how to give good things to your children. How much more will your Father in heaven give good things to those who ask Him?

Kid-Builder Value
TRUST is an unwavering belief in someone or something, especially in regard to truth, strength, or character. To put your trust in God means to rely on Him to provide everything you need.

KID-BUILDER Questions

- Read the Lord's Prayer (verses 9-13). How does prayer show trust in God? How is this prayer an example of trust?

- Ask, look, and knock, are word pictures to help people understand that they are to keep praying. "To look" in this case means that you are trusting that God will answer your prayer. What can you ask for or look for?

- While we're trusting God for our needs, He wants us to work to build His kingdom. What can you do to help build God's kingdom?

KID-BUILDER Prayer

Lord, thank You for providing the things I need. Help me to talk to You in prayer every day.

In Jesus' name. Amen.

Memory Verse:

Learn to pray about everything. Give thanks to God as you ask Him for what you need.   Phil 4:6b

Throughout Scripture, we read verses that show us that prayer is important to God. He wants us to build a relationship with Him by talking to Him on a regular basis. You can't have a friendship when one person is doing all the talking—it takes talking and listening on the part of both people to make a friendship.

How do you talk to God? Jesus' disciples had the same question. They asked Him to teach them how to pray. He taught them by giving them an example. We call it the Lord's Prayer (Matthew 6:9-13). You can use this prayer to build your confidence in talking to God. Soon you will want to use your own words. The most important thing is that you start talking to God and building your relationship with Him today.

Here are a few pointers to keep in mind:

- *Don't* show off when you pray. Prayer is a way of getting close to God, not of impressing other people.
- *Do* talk to God by yourself in a quiet place—like your own room. What you say can be a secret between the two of you.
- *Do* think when you pray. Prayer is not just mumbling words that you've memorized. Prayer is talking to a special person.
- *Don't* worry about getting God's attention. He already knows what you need, and He's eager to listen to you.
- *Don't* give up if your prayers aren't answered right away or if they aren't answered in the way you want.
- *Do* keep praying. God will answer in the best way at the best time.
- *Do* pray with other people in addition to praying by yourself. Jesus promised that whenever Christians gather to pray to Him, He will be right there with them (Matt. 18:20).
- *Do* believe that God is your loving heavenly Father who wants to give you His good gifts (Matt. 7:11).

MATTHEW

An Army Captain Shows Faith in Jesus

Matthew 8

Jesus came to the city of Capernaum. A captain of the army came to Him. He asked for help, ⁶saying, "Lord, my helper boy is sick in bed. He is not able to move his body. He is in much pain." ⁷Jesus said to the captain, "I will come and heal him." ⁸The captain said, "Lord, I am not good enough for You to come to my house. Only speak the word, and my helper boy will be healed. ⁹I am a man who works for someone else and I have men working under me. I say to this man, 'Go!' and he goes. I say to another, 'Come!' and he comes. I say to my servant, 'Do this!' and he does it."

¹⁰When Jesus heard this, He was surprised and wondered about it. He said to those who followed Him, "For sure, I tell you, I have not found so

Kid-Builder Value
FAITH is the act of believing the things that God has revealed about Himself and acting on those beliefs. The captain showed faith in Jesus when he asked Him to heal his servant.

much faith in the Jewish nation. . . ." [13]Jesus said to the captain, "Go your way. It is done for you even as you had faith to believe." The helper boy was healed at that time.

KID-BUILDER Questions

- What did the captain want Jesus to do?

- What do you think Jesus would say about your faith? What would you want Him to say?

- In what ways have you acted on your faith in the past? the present?

KID-BUILDER Prayer

Lord, I trust You to provide for my needs. Thank You for what You do for me each day.

In Jesus' name. Amen.

Memory Verse:
If you have faith as a mustard seed, you will say to this mountain, "Move from here to over there," and it would move over. You will be able to do anything.   Matt. 17:20b

MATTHEW

Jesus' Arrest and Crucifixion

Matthew 26—27

Judas Iscariot was one of the twelve followers. He went to the religious leaders of the Jews. 15He said, "What will you pay me if I hand Jesus over to you?" They promised to pay him thirty pieces of silver. 16From that time on Judas looked for a way to hand Jesus over to them. . . .

36Jesus came with [the followers] to a place called Gethsemane. He said to them, "You sit here while I go over there to pray." 37He took Peter and the two sons of Zebedee with Him. . . . 38Then He said to them, "My soul . . . is so full of sorrow I am ready to die. You stay here and watch with Me."

39He went on a little farther and got down with His face on the ground. He prayed, "My Father, if it can be done, take away what is before Me. Even so, not what I want but what You want."

40Then He came to the followers and found them sleeping. He said to Peter, "Were you not able to watch with Me one hour? 41Watch and pray so that you will not be tempted. Man's spirit is willing, but the body does not have the power to do it."

42He went away again the second time. He prayed, saying, "My Father, if this must happen to Me, may whatever You want be done." 43He came and found them asleep again. . . .

47Judas . . . came with many others who had swords and sticks. . . . 49At once Judas went up to Jesus and said, "Hello, Teacher," and kissed Him. 50 Jesus said to him, "Friend, do what you came to do." Then they came and put their hands on Jesus and took Him. . . . Then all the followers left Him and ran away.

57Those who had taken Jesus led Him away to Caiaphas. He was the head religious leader. . . . 59The . . . leaders and all the court were looking for false things to say against Jesus. They wanted some reason to kill Him. 60They found none, but many came and told false things about Him. . . .

27:1Early in the morning all the head religious leaders of the Jews and the leaders of the people gathered together and talked about how they could put Jesus to death. 2 . . . Then they handed

Kid-Builder Fact
Matt. 27:35 Crucifixion (kroo-suh-FIX-shun) was the kind of death Jesus suffered to make salvation possible for us. It was a terribly painful way to die. Romans used crucifixion to execute criminals who were not citizens of Rome. Hands and feet were nailed to the wood, and the person was left to hang there until he suffocated. Death usually took two to eight days, but Jesus died in a few hours.

Him over to Pilate who was the leader of the country. . . . [11][Pilate] asked Jesus, "Are You the King of the Jews?" Jesus said to him, "What you say is true." [12]When the . . . leaders spoke against Him, He said nothing. . . .

[15]At the special supper each year the leader of the country would always let one person who was in prison go free. It would be the one the people wanted. [16]They had a man who was known by all the people whose name was Barabbas. . . .

[20]The head religious leaders and the other leaders talked the many people into asking for Barabbas to go free and for Jesus to be put to death. [21][Pilate] said to them, "Which one of the two do you want me to let go free?" They said, "Barabbas." [22]Pilate said to them, "Then what am I to do with Jesus Who is called Christ?" They all said to him, "Nail Him to a cross!" . . .

[24]Pilate . . . took water and washed his hands in front of the many people. He said, "I am not guilty of the blood of this good Man. This is your own doing." [25]Then all the people said, "Let His blood be on us and on our children!" [26]Pilate let Barabbas go free but he had men whip Jesus. Then he handed Him over to be nailed to a cross.

[27]Then the soldiers of Pilate took Jesus into a large room. . . . [28]They took off His clothes and put a purple coat on Him. [29]They put a crown of thorns on His head. They put a stick in His right hand. . . .

[31] . . . Then they led Him away to be nailed to a cross. [32]As they were on the way, they came to a man called Simon from the country of Cyrene. They made him carry the cross for Jesus.

[33]They came to a place called Golgotha. This name means the place of a skull. . . . [35]When they had nailed Him to the cross, they divided His clothes by drawing names. . . . [37]Over His head they put in writing what they had against Him, THIS IS JESUS THE KING OF THE JEWS.

[38]They nailed two robbers to crosses beside Him. . . . [39]Those who walked by shook their heads and laughed at Him. . . .

[41]The . . . leaders and the teachers of the Law and the other leaders made fun of Him also. They said, [42]"He saved others but He cannot save Himself. If He is the King of the Jews, let Him come down from the cross. Then we will believe in Him." . . .

[45]From noon until three o'clock it was dark over all the land. [46]About three o'clock Jesus cried with a loud voice, "My God, My God, why have You left Me alone?" . . . [48]At once one of [the bystanders] . . . took a sponge and filled it with sour wine. He

Kid-Builder Value
REPENTANCE is sorrow for one's sin, and it is a turning away from that sin to serve God and do right. Judas repented, but it was too late for him. It's not too late for you. Because of Jesus' death on the cross, repentance is possible for everyone who is willing to turn to God.

put it on a stick and gave it to Him to drink. . . . 50Then Jesus gave another loud cry and . . . died.

51At once the curtain in the house of God was torn in two from top to bottom. The earth shook and the rocks fell apart. 52Graves were opened. Bodies of many of God's people who were dead were raised. . . .

54The captain of the soldiers and those with him who were watching Jesus, saw all the things that were happening. . . . They said, "For sure, this Man was the Son of God." . . .

57When it was evening, a rich man came from the city of Arimathea. His name was Joseph. He was a follower of Jesus also. 58He went to Pilate and asked for the body of Jesus. . . . 59Joseph took the body and put clean linen cloth around it. 60He laid it in his own new grave. This grave had been cut out in the side of a rock. He pushed a big stone over the door of the grave and went away. . . .

62The next day, . . . the head religious leaders and the proud religious law-keepers gathered together in front of Pilate. 63They said, ". . . 64Speak the word to have the grave watched for three days. Then His followers cannot come at night and take Him away." . . . 65Pilate said to them, "Take the soldiers. Go and watch the grave." 66Then they went and made the soldiers stand by the grave. They put a lock on the big stone door.

KID-BUILDER Questions

- What did Jesus ask God from the cross?

- What does repentance mean to you?
  Why is repentance necessary?

- Have you ever felt that God doesn't care about you?
  Think about Jesus' sacrificial act. How does that
  show God's concern for you? How does it show
  God's dislike of sin?

KID-BUILDER Prayer

*Lord, I thank You that Jesus was willing to pay the
price for my sin.*   *In Jesus' name. Amen.*

Memory Verse:
Christ suffered and died for sins once for all. He never sinned and
yet He died for us who have sinned. He died so He might bring us
to God.   I Pet. 3:18a

MARK

Mark is written by John Mark, who traveled with the apostle Paul. Mark begins his story when Jesus was thirty years old, and tells us about what Jesus does rather than what He says.

Jesus Heals a Paralyzed Man

Mark 2

After some days Jesus went back to the city of Capernaum. Then news got around that He was home. ²Soon many people gathered there. There was no more room, not even at the door. He spoke the Word of God to them. ³Four men came to Jesus carrying a man who could not move his body. ⁴These men could not get near Jesus because of so many people. They made a hole in the roof of the house over where Jesus stood. Then they let down the bed with the sick man on it.

Kid-Builder Fact
Mark 2:4 In Bible times, the roofs of houses were flat. There was no need for a slanting roof in a land with so little rain. The roofs could be used for extra sleeping space, for drying flax, and for other activities. Stone steps often led from the courtyard to the roof.

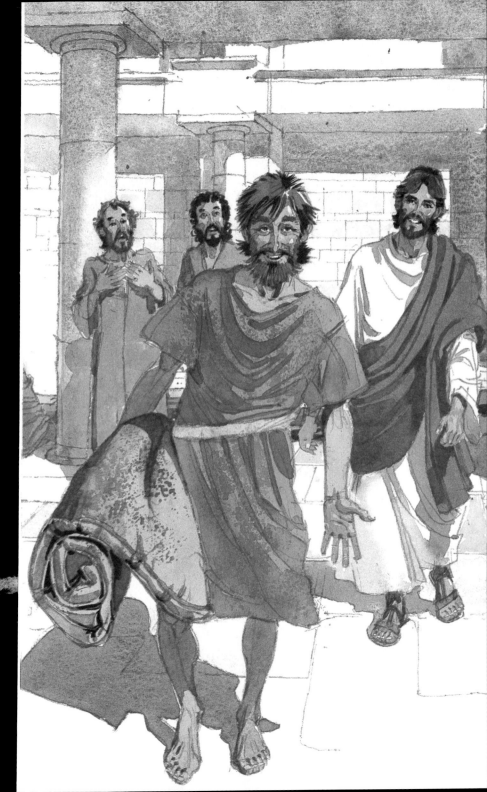

5When Jesus saw their faith, He said to the sick man, "Son, your sins are forgiven." 6Some teachers of the Law were sitting there. They thought to themselves, 7"Why does this Man talk like this? He is speaking as if He is God! Who can forgive sins? Only One can forgive sins and that is God!"

8At once Jesus knew the teachers of the Law were thinking this. He said to them, "Why do you think this in your hearts? 9Which is easier to say to the sick man, 'Your sins are forgiven,' or to say, 'Get up, take your bed, and start to walk?' 10I am doing this so you may know the Son of Man has power on earth to forgive sins." He said to the sick man who could not move his body, 11"I say to you, 'Get up. Take your bed and go to your home.' " 12At once the sick man got up and took his bed and went away. Everybody saw him. They were all surprised and wondered about it. They thanked God, saying, "We have never seen anything like this!"

Kid-Builder Value
RESPONSIBILITY means you are able and willing to do what you say you'll do. The four men took responsibility for their sick friend.

• •

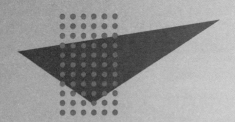

KID-BUILDER Questions

- The four men felt responsible for their friend. What responsibilities do you have toward your friends and family?

- Are there any responsibilities that you feel are too big for you? What kind of help would you need or want?

KID-BUILDER Prayer

Lord, help me do my best in everything.
In Jesus' name. Amen.

Memory Verse:
Help each other in troubles and problems. This is the kind of law Christ asks us to obey.   Gal. 6:2

MARK

Jairus's Daughter

Mark 5

Jesus went over to the other side of the sea by boat. Many people gathered around Him. He stayed by the seashore. 22Jairus was one of the leaders of the Jewish place of worship. As Jairus

came to Jesus, he got down at His feet. 23He cried out to Jesus and said, "My little daughter is almost dead. Come and put your hand on her that she may be healed and live." 24Jesus went with him. Many people followed and pushed around Jesus. . . .

35While Jesus spoke, men came from the house of the leader of the place of worship. They said, "Your daughter is dead. Why trouble the Teacher anymore?" 36Jesus heard this. He said to the leader of the Jewish place of worship, "Do not be afraid, just believe." 37He allowed no one to go with Him but Peter and James and John, the brother of James. 38They came to the house where the leader

of the place of worship lived. Jesus found many people making much noise and crying. 39He went in and asked them, "Why is there so much noise and crying? The girl is not dead. She is sleeping."

40They laughed at Jesus. But He sent them all out of the room. Then He took the girl's father and mother and those who were with Him. They went into the room where the girl was. 41He took the girl by the hand and said, "Little girl, I say to you, get up!" 42At once the girl got up and walked. She was twelve years old. They were very much surprised and wondered about it. 43He spoke sharp words to them that they should not tell anyone. He told them to give her something to eat.

KID-BUILDER Questions

- It's easy to laugh at something someone says he'll do if you don't trust that person to keep his word. How do you feel when someone makes a promise to you and doesn't keep it?

- What does it mean to trust someone? How do you build trust in someone?

KID-BUILDER Prayer

Lord, I know You want us to trust You. But I don't always know how. Help me have confidence in You.
                              In Jesus' name. Amen.

Memory Verse:
May He fill you with joy and peace because of your trust in Him.
                              Romans 15:13b

MARK

Triumphal Entry

Mark 11

Jesus and His followers were near Jerusalem at the Mount of Olives. They were in the towns of Bethphage and Bethany. Jesus sent two of His followers on ahead. ²He said to them, "Go into the town over there. As soon as you get there, you will find a young donkey tied. No man has ever sat on it. Let the donkey loose and bring it here. ³If anyone asks you, 'Why are you doing that?' say, 'The Lord needs it. He will send it back again soon.'"

⁴The two followers went on their way. They found the young donkey tied by the door where two streets crossed. They took the rope off its neck. ⁵Some men were standing there. They said to the two followers, "Why are you taking the rope off that young donkey?" ⁶The two followers told them what Jesus had said and the men let them take the donkey. ⁷They brought it to Jesus and put their coats over it. Jesus sat on the donkey. ⁸Many people put their clothes down on the road. Others cut branches off the trees and put them down on

the road. [9]Those who went in front and those who followed spoke with loud voices. "Greatest One! Great and honored is He Who comes in the name of the Lord! [10]Great is the coming holy nation of our father David. It will come in the name of the Lord, Greatest One in the highest heaven."

11Jesus came to Jerusalem and went into the house of God. He looked around at everything. Then He went with the twelve followers to the town of Bethany because it was late. . . .

15Then they came to Jerusalem. Jesus went into the house of God. He began to make the people leave who were selling and buying in the house of God. He turned over the tables of the men who changed money. He turned over the seats of those who sold doves. 16He would not allow anyone to carry a pot or pan through the house of God. 17He taught them saying, "Is it not written, 'My house is to be called a house of prayer for all the nations'? You have made it a place of robbers."

18The teachers of the Law and the religious leaders of the Jews heard it. They tried to find some way to put Jesus to death. But they were afraid of Him because all the people were surprised and wondered about His teaching.

Kid-Builder Value
REVERENCE is a feeling of deep respect mixed with wonder, fear, and love. The people showed reverence for Jesus when He entered Jerusalem. Jesus showed reverence for God's house by driving the money changers out of the temple.

KID-BUILDER Questions

- How did the people show their reverence for Jesus? Why does Jesus deserve reverence?

- How does your attitude toward God's house show reverence? In what ways could you improve? Who would you say you're more like: the people who welcomed Jesus to Jerusalem or the money changers? Why?

KID-BUILDER Prayer

Lord, help me show respect for You by having a good attitude toward Your house—the church, my Bible, and my pastor. *In Jesus' name. Amen.*

Memory Verse:
Keep My Days of Rest and honor My holy place. I am the Lord.

Lev. 19:30

MARK

Peter's Denial

Mark 14

Jesus was arrested and led away to stand trial. Peter decided to follow to see what would happen to Jesus.

Jesus said to them [at the Last Supper], "All of you will be ashamed of Me and leave Me tonight. . . ." ²⁹Peter said to Him, "Even if all men are ashamed of You and leave You, I never will." ³⁰Jesus said to him, "For sure, I tell you, that today, even tonight, before a rooster crows two times, you will say three times you do not know Me." ³¹Peter spoke with strong words, "Even if I have to die with You, I will never say that I do not know You." All the followers said the same thing. . . .

⁶⁶Peter was outside in the yard. One of the servant-girls of the head religious leader came. ⁶⁷She saw Peter getting warm. She looked at him and

> **Kid-Builder Value**
> **FAITHFULNESS** means being loyal or "full of faith."
> Peter's denial showed a lack of faithfulness in the middle of a crisis.

said, "You were with Jesus of Nazareth." 68Peter lied, saying, "I do not know Jesus and do not understand what you are talking about." As he went out, a rooster crowed.

69The servant-girl saw him again. She said to the people standing around, "This man is one of them." 70He lied again saying that he did not know Jesus. Later, those who stood around said to Peter again, "For sure you are one of them. You are from the country of Galilee. You talk like they do." 71He began to say strong words and to swear. He said, "I do not know the Man you are talking about!"

72At once a rooster crowed the second time. Peter remembered what Jesus had said to him, "Before a rooster crows two times, you will say three times you do not know Me." When he thought about it, he cried.

KID-BUILDER Questions

- How do you think Peter felt? How would you feel in that same situation?

- Have there been times when you failed to be faithful? What happened?

KID-BUILDER Prayer

Lord, thank You for being faithful, even when I am not.   *In Jesus' name. Amen.*

Memory Verse:
O Lord, Your loving-kindness goes to the heavens. You are as faithful as the sky is high.   Ps. 36:5

LUKE

Luke is written by Luke, a Gentile doctor. He was not one of the twelve followers specially chosen by Jesus, but was a friend of the apostle Paul. He begins his book with the birth of John the Baptist, Jesus' cousin.

Birth Announcements

Luke 1

When Herod was king of the country of Judea, there was a Jewish religious leader named Zacharias. . . . His wife was of the family group of Aaron. Her name was Elizabeth. 6They were right with God and obeyed the Jewish Law. . . . 7They had no children because Elizabeth was not able to have a child. Both of them were older people.

8Zacharias was doing his work as a religious leader for God. 9The religious leaders were given certain kinds of work to do. Zacharias was chosen to go to the house of God to burn special perfume. . . .

11Zacharias saw an angel of the Lord standing on the right side of the altar where the special perfume was burning. [12]When he saw the angel, Zacharias was troubled and afraid. [13]The angel said to him, "Zacharias, do not be afraid. Your prayer has been heard. Your wife Elizabeth will give birth to a son. You are to name him John. . . . [15]He will be great in the sight of the Lord and will never drink wine or any strong drink. Even from his birth, he will be filled with the Holy Spirit. . . . [17]. . . He will get people ready for the Lord."

[18]Zacharias said to the angel, "How can I know this for sure? I am old and my wife is old also." [19]The angel said to him, "My name is Gabriel. I stand near God. He sent me to talk to you and bring to you this good news. [20]See! You will not be able to talk until the day this happens. It is because you did not believe my words. . . ."

[21]The people outside . . . wondered why Zacharias stayed so long in the house of God. [22]When he came out, he could not talk to them. . . .

[26]Six months after Elizabeth knew she was to become a mother, Gabriel was sent from God to Nazareth. Nazareth was a town in the country of Galilee. [27]He went to a woman [whose] . . . name was Mary. She was promised in marriage to a man

Kid-Builder Value
JOYFULNESS is an intense feeling of good. Mary, Elizabeth, and Zacharias were made joyful at the angel's announcements.

named Joseph. Joseph was of the family of David. ²⁸The angel came to her and said, "You are . . . a favored woman. The Lord is with you. . . ."

²⁹When she saw the angel, she was troubled at his words. She thought about what had been said. ³⁰The angel said to her, "Mary, do not be afraid. You have found favor with God. ³¹See! You are to become a mother and have a Son. You are to give Him the name Jesus. ³²He will be great. He will be called the Son of the Most High. . . . ³³He will be King over the family of Jacob forever and His nation will have no end."

³⁴Mary said to the angel, "How can this happen? I have never had a man." ³⁵The angel said to her, "The Holy Spirit will come on

you. . . . The holy Child you give birth to will be called the Son of God.

36"See, your cousin Elizabeth, as old as she is, is going to give birth to a child. She was not able to have children before, but now she is in her sixth month. 37For God can do all things." 38Then Mary said, "I am willing to be used of the Lord. Let it happen to me as you have said." Then the angel went away from her.

39At once Mary went from there to a town in the hill country of Judea. 40She went to the house of Zacharias to see Elizabeth. ⁴¹When Elizabeth heard Mary speak, the baby moved in her body. At the same time Elizabeth was filled with the Holy Spirit.

⁴²Elizabeth spoke in a loud voice, "You are honored among women! Your Child is honored! . . . ⁴⁴As soon as I heard your voice, the baby in my body moved for joy. ⁴⁵Everything will happen as the Lord told you it would happen."

⁴⁶Then Mary said, "My heart sings with thanks for my Lord. . . . ⁴⁸The Lord has looked on me, the one He owns and the one who is not important. But from now on all people will honor me. ⁴⁹He Who is powerful has done great things for me. His name is holy. ⁵⁰The loving-pity of the Lord is given to the people of all times who honor Him. . . ."
⁵⁶Mary stayed with Elizabeth about three months. Then she went to her own home.

⁵⁷When the time came, Elizabeth gave birth to a son. ⁵⁸Her neighbors and family heard how the Lord had shown loving-pity to her. They were happy for her. ⁵⁹On the eighth day they did the religious act of the Jews on the child. They named him Zacharias, after his father. ⁶⁰But his mother said, "No! His name is John." ⁶¹They said to her, "No one in your family has that name."

⁶²Then they talked to his father with their hands to find out what he would name the child. ⁶³He asked for something to write on.

● ●

He wrote, "His name is John." They were all surprised and wondered about it. 64Zacharias was able to talk from that time on and he gave thanks to God. . . .

80The child grew and became strong in spirit. He lived in a desert until the day he started to preach to the Jews.

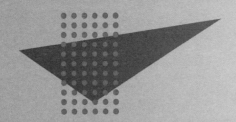

KID-BUILDER Questions

- How did Mary, Zacharias, and Elizabeth express their joy?

- Think about a time when you felt joyful. What was the cause?

- Think about the words to the song "Joy to the World!" What do they express? How can you put that in your own words?

KID-BUILDER Prayer

Lord, the promise of Jesus makes my heart glad. Thank You for sending Him to bring lasting joy to my life.   *In Jesus' name. Amen.*

Memory Verse:
Be glad as you serve the Lord. Come before Him with songs of joy.
Ps. 100:2

Jesus Is Born

Luke 2

In those days Caesar Augustus sent out word that the name of every person in the Roman nation must be written in the books of the nation. 2This first writing took place while Quirinius was leader of Syria.

3So all the people went to their own cities to have their names written in the books of the nation. 4Joseph went up from the town of Nazareth in the country of Galilee to the town of Bethlehem. It was known as the city of David. He went there because he was from the family of David. 5Joseph went to have his and Mary's names written in the books of the nation. Mary was his promised wife and soon to become a mother.

6While they were there in Bethlehem, the time came for Mary to give birth to her baby. 7Her first son was born. She put cloth around Him and laid Him in a place where cattle are fed. There was no room for them in the place where people stay for the night.

⁸In the same country there were shepherds in the fields. They were watching their flocks of sheep at night. ⁹The angel of the Lord came to them. The shining greatness of the Lord shone around them. They were very much afraid. ¹⁰The angel said to them, "Do not be afraid. See! I bring you good news of great joy which is for all people. ¹¹Today, One Who saves from the punishment of sin has been born in the city of David. He is Christ the Lord. ¹²There will be something special for you to see. This is the way you will know Him. You

will find the Baby with cloth around Him, lying in a place where cattle are fed."

13At once many angels from heaven were seen, along with the angel, giving thanks to God. They were saying, 14"Greatness and honor to our God in the highest heaven and peace on earth among men who please Him."

15The angels went from the shepherds back to heaven. The shepherds said to each other, "Let us go to Bethlehem and see what has happened. The Lord has told us about this." 16They went fast and found Mary and Joseph. They found the Baby lying in a place where cattle are fed. 17When they saw the Child, they told what the angel said about Him. 18All who heard it were surprised at what the shepherds told them. 19But Mary hid all these words in her heart. She thought about them much. 20The shepherds went back full of joy. They thanked God for all they had heard and seen. It happened as the angel had told them.

Kid-Builder Value
PRAISE includes words or actions that give honor to someone. The angels and shepherds praised God at the birth of the Savior.

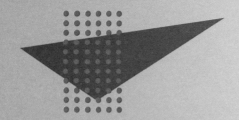

KID-BUILDER Questions

- The Savior's birth had been announced hundreds of years previous to His birth. His arrival was big news, deserving of praise. If you had been with the shepherds, how would you have praised God?

- Praise starts with a thankful heart. For what are you thankful? How can you turn that into praise?

KID-BUILDER Prayer

Lord, the everyday things in life remind me to praise You: the sunlight, the flowers, and my family and friends.   *In Jesus' name. Amen.*

Memory Verse:
he Lord is great and our praise to Him should be great. He is too great for anyone to understand.   Ps. 145:3

LUKE

Jesus Talks to the Temple Leaders

Luke 2

When Joseph and Mary had done everything the Law said to do, they went back to Nazareth in Galilee. 40The Child grew and became strong in spirit. He was filled with wisdom and the loving-favor of God was on Him.

41His parents went to Jerusalem every year for the special religious gathering to remember how the Jews left Egypt. 42When He was twelve years old, they went up to Jerusalem as they had done before. 43When the days of the special supper were over, they started back to their town. But the boy Jesus was still in Jerusalem. His parents did not know it. 44They thought Jesus was with the others of the group. They walked for one day. Then they looked for Him among their family and friends.

45When they could not find Jesus, they turned back to Jerusalem to look for Him. 46Three days later they found Him in the house of God. He was sitting among the teachers. He was hearing what they said and asking questions. 47All those who

heard Him were surprised and wondered about His understanding and at what He said. ⁴⁸When His parents saw Him, they were surprised. His mother said to Him, "My Son, why have You done this to us? See! Your father and I have had much sorrow looking for

You." ⁴⁹He said to them, "Why were you looking for Me? Do you not know that I must be in My Father's house?" ⁵⁰They did not understand the things He said to them.

⁵¹He went with them to Nazareth and obeyed them. But His mother kept all these words in her heart. ⁵²Jesus grew strong in mind and body. He grew in favor with God and men.

Kid-Builder Value
CONCERN is a feeling of anxiety, or interest in, someone else. Mary and Joseph were concerned when they could not find Jesus. Loving parents are a blessing.

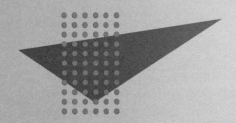

KID-BUILDER Questions

- What did Mary and Joseph do when they discovered Jesus was missing?

- Did you ever do something that caused your parents to worry? How did they react?

- Why is obedience to parents important?

KID-BUILDER Prayer

Lord, I don't always obey, but I want to be obedient. In Jesus' name. Amen.

Memory Verse:
Children, as Christians, obey your parents. This is the right thing to do.   Eph. 6:1

LUKE

Jesus Calms a Storm

Luke 8

Jesus and His followers got into a boat. Jesus said to them, "Let us go over to the other side of the lake." Then they pushed out into the water. 23As they were going, Jesus fell asleep. A wind storm came over the lake. The boat was filling with water and they were in danger. 24The followers came to awake Jesus. They said, "Teacher! Teacher! We are going to die!" Then Jesus got up and spoke sharp words to the wind and the high waves. The wind stopped blowing and there were no more waves. 25He said to them, "Where is your faith?" The followers were surprised and afraid. They said to each other, "What kind of a man is He? He speaks to the wind and the waves and they obey Him."

Kid-Builder Value
PEACEFULNESS is the sense of being at rest even though you may be experiencing a scary situation. Jesus brought peace to the storm. He can also bring peace to your life.

KID-BUILDER Questions

- Think about a time you felt really scared, then felt peaceful. What's the difference between those two feelings?

- What stormy circumstances are you facing? Think about how God brought peace in the past. If Jesus was powerful enough to stop a storm, what do you think He can do with your situation?

KID-BUILDER Prayer

Lord, I need Your peace in my life.
                              In Jesus' name. Amen.

Memory Verse:
I give you My peace and leave it with you. I do not give peace to you as the world gives. Do not let your hearts be troubled or afraid.
                                                    John 14:27

LUKE

The Good Samaritan

Luke 10

A man stood up who knew the Law and tried to trap Jesus. He said, "Teacher, what must I do to have life that lasts forever?" 26Jesus said to him, "What is written in the Law? What does the Law say?" 27The man said, "You must love the Lord your God with all your heart. You must love Him with all your soul. You must love Him with all your strength. You must love Him with all your mind. You must love your neighbor as you love yourself." 28Jesus said to him, "You have said the right thing. Do this and you will have life." 29The man tried to make himself look good. He asked Jesus, "Who is my neighbor?"

30Jesus said, "A man was going down from Jerusalem to the city of Jericho. Robbers came out after him. They took his clothes off and beat him. Then they went away, leaving him almost dead. 31A religious leader was walking down that road and saw the man. But he went by on the other side. 32In the same way, a man from the family group of Levi

was walking down that road. When he saw the man who was hurt, he came near to him but kept on going on the other side of the road. ³³Then a man from the country of Samaria came by. He went up to the man. As he saw him, he had loving-pity on him. ³⁴He got down and put oil and wine on the places where he was hurt and put cloth around them. Then the man from Samaria put this man on his own donkey. He took him to a place where people stay for the night and cared for him. ³⁵The next day the man from Samaria was ready to leave. He gave the owner of that place two pieces of money to care for him. He said to him, 'Take care of this man. If you use more than this, I will give it to you when I come again.'

³⁶"Which of these three do you think was a neighbor to the man who was beaten by the robbers?" ³⁷The man who knew the Law said, "The one who showed loving-pity on him." Then Jesus said, "Go and do the same."

Kid-Builder Value
COMPASSION is a combination of love, care, and the desire to help. The Samaritan in Jesus' parable showed compassion to someone in need. We can show compassion to others by what we do or say.

KID-BUILDER Questions

- What do you think Jesus wanted His listeners (including you) to learn from this story?

- Suppose someone you didn't get along with very well was hurt. How can the Samaritan's example help you show compassion?

- Was there a time when you needed someone's help and couldn't get it? How did you feel?

KID-BUILDER Prayer

Lord, help me see the needs of others and how I can meet those needs.   *In Jesus' name. Amen.*

Memory Verse:
You must love your neighbor as you love yourself.   Luke 10:27

• •

LUKE

The Prodigal Son

Luke 15

All the tax gatherers and sinners were coming to hear Jesus. ²The proud religious law-keepers and the teachers of the Law began to speak against Him. They said, "This man receives sinners and eats with them."

³Then Jesus told them a picture-story. . . . ¹¹Jesus said, "There was a man who had two sons. ¹²The younger son said to his father, 'Father, let me have the part of the family riches that will be coming to me.' Then the father divided all that he owned between his two sons. ¹³Soon after that the younger son took all that had been given to him and went to another country far away. There he spent all he had on wild and foolish living. ¹⁴When

Kid-Builder Fact
Luke 15:22 A ring symbolized special authority in ancient times. Each household had a ring that represented the authority of that household. When the father in this story placed the ring on the hand of his son, it showed that the son was fully restored to his place of authority in the family.

all his money was spent, he was hungry. There was no food in the land. ¹⁵He went to work for a man in this far away country. His work was to feed pigs. ¹⁶He was so hungry he was ready to eat the outside part of the ears of the corn the pigs ate because no one gave him anything.

[17]"He began to think about what he had done. He said to himself, 'My father pays many men who work for him. They have all the food they want and more than enough. I am about dead because I am so hungry. [18]I will get up and go to my father. I will say to him, "Father, I have sinned against heaven and against you. [19]I am not good enough to be called your son. But may I be as one of the workmen you pay to work?"'

[20]"The son got up and went to his father. While he was yet a long way off, his father saw him. The

father was full of loving-pity for him. He ran and
threw his arms around him and kissed him. 21The
son said to him, 'Father, I have sinned against
heaven and against you. I am not good enough to
be called your son.' 22But the father said to the
workmen he owned, 'Hurry! Get the best coat and
put it on him. Put a ring on his hand and shoes on
his feet. 23Bring the calf that is fat and kill it. Let us
eat and be glad. 24For my son was dead and now he
is alive again. He was lost and now he is found. Let
us eat and have a good time.' . . ."

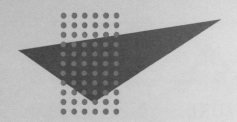

KID-BUILDER Questions

- Why did the son leave home?

- Have you ever wished you could do whatever you wanted to do? What are some drawbacks to always getting what you want?

- Jesus wanted people to know that God is like that kind father in the story. Is that how you picture God in your mind? Why or why not?

KID-BUILDER Prayer

Lord, I'm glad that You're willing to take me back when I stray.   In Jesus' name. Amen.

Memory Verse:
The Lord does not want any person to be punished forever. He wants all people to be sorry for their sins and turn from them.

II Pet 3:9b

LUKE

Ten Lepers

Luke 17

Jesus went on His way to Jerusalem. He was passing between the countries of Samaria and Galilee. 12As He was going into one of the towns, ten men with a bad skin disease came to Him. They stood a little way off. 13They called to Him, "Jesus! Teacher! Take pity on us!" 14When Jesus saw them, He said, "Go and show yourselves to the religious leaders." As they went, they were healed. 15One of them turned back when he saw he was healed. He thanked God with a loud voice. 16He got down on his face at the feet of Jesus and thanked Him. He was from . . . Samaria. 17Jesus asked, "Were there not ten men who were healed? Where are the other nine? 18Is this stranger from

Kid-Builder Value
THANKFULNESS is recognizing that God created everything and telling Him "thank you" for all He has done. One man gave thanks to Jesus for healing him.

another country the only one
who turned back to give
thanks to God?" ¹⁹Then Jesus
said to him, "Get up and go
on your way. Your trust in
God has healed you."

KID-BUILDER Questions

- How many lepers did Jesus heal? How many returned to thank Him?

- Has there ever been a time when someone forgot to thank you for a gift or a favor? How did you feel?

- There are some things God gives us every day that we all take for granted. How often do you thank Him for the warm sunlight; the seasons; the love of your family, friends, and pets?

KID-BUILDER Prayer

Lord, thank You for what You have done for me. Help me to have a grateful heart.   In Jesus' name. Amen.

Memory Verse:
Give thanks to the Lord for He is good! His loving-kindness lasts forever!   Ps. 107:1

JOHN

John was written by the apostle John, when he was old. John wanted people to know that Jesus was the Son of God, the Savior God had promised to send long ago.

Jesus Calls Disciples to Follow Him

John 1

John the Baptist was standing with two of his own followers. 36Jesus walked by. John looked at Him and said, "See! The Lamb of God." 37John's two followers heard him say this and followed Jesus. . . . 40Andrew, Simon Peter's brother, was one of the two who had heard John's words and had followed Jesus. 41The first thing he did was to find his brother Simon. He said to him, "We have found the Christ!" 42Andrew took Simon to Jesus. When Jesus saw Simon, He said, "You are Simon, the son of John. Your name will be Cephas." The

Kid-Builder Fact
John 1:44 Bethsaida was a fishing village on the northwestern shores of Lake Galilee.

name Cephas means Peter, or a rock.

⁴³The next day Jesus wanted to go to the country of Galilee. He found Philip and said to him, "Follow Me." ⁴⁴Philip was from the town of Bethsaida. Andrew and Peter were from this town also. ⁴⁵Philip found Nathanael and said to him, "We have found the One Moses wrote about in the Law. He is the One the early preachers wrote about. He is Jesus of Nazareth, the Son of Joseph." ⁴⁶Nathanael said, "Can anything good come out of the town of Nazareth?" Philip said, "Come and see."

Kid-Builder Fact
John 1:46 Nazareth was the town in Galilee where Jesus lived during His childhood and youth. Jews who lived in other places thought Nazareth was a city of low moral and religious standards.

⁴⁷Jesus saw Nathanael coming to Him and said, "See! There is a true Jew. There is nothing false in him." ⁴⁸Nathanael said to Jesus, "How do You know me?" Jesus answered him, "Before Philip talked to you, I saw you under the fig tree." ⁴⁹Nathanael said to Him, "Teacher, You are the Son of God. You are the King of the Jews." ⁵⁰Jesus said to him, "Do you believe because I said I saw you under the fig tree? You will see greater things than that."

Kid-Builder Value

FAITH is the act of believing the things that God has revealed about Himself and acting on those beliefs. Andrew, Philip, Peter, and Nathanael were Jewish men who had been waiting for God to send a Savior. John the Baptist helped to point them to Jesus. They believed that Jesus was the Savior. By faith they left everything to follow Jesus at the beginning of His public ministry.

KID-BUILDER Questions

- Is there someone you admire? How would you feel if you had a chance to meet that person? Andrew, Peter, Philip, and Nathanael were so thrilled to meet Jesus that they gave up everything to follow Him. What does that tell you about Jesus?

- Andrew and Philip each brought someone to Jesus. How could you share your faith in Jesus with a friend?

KID-BUILDER Prayer

Lord, help me believe that Jesus is the Savior You promised to send. Help me follow Him like Andrew, Philip, Peter, and Nathanael did.

In Jesus' name. Amen.

Memory Verse:
Simon Peter said, "You are the Christ, the Son of the living God."
Matt. 16:16

JOHN

Miracle at a Wedding

John 2

There was a wedding in the town of Cana in the country of Galilee. The mother of Jesus was there. 2Jesus and His followers were asked to come to the wedding. 3When the wine was all gone, the mother of Jesus said to Him, "They have no more wine." 4Jesus said to her, "Woman, what is that to you and to Me. It is not time for Me to work yet." 5His mother said to the helpers, "Do whatever He says."

6Six stone water jars were there. Each one held about one-half barrel of water. These water jars were used in the Jewish worship of washing. 7Jesus said to the helpers, "Fill the jars with water." They filled them to the top. 8Then He said, "Take some out and give it to the head man who is caring

Kid-Builder Fact
John 2:6 Water jars were clay pitchers used in ancient times by people who had to haul water from wells or springs to their houses or troughs. Each clay pot held from 20 to 30 gallons.

for the people." They took some to him. ⁹The head man tasted the water that had become wine. He did not know where it came from but the helpers who took it to him knew. He called the man who had just been married. ¹⁰The head man said to him, "Everyone puts out his best wine first. After people have had much to drink, he puts out the wine that is not so good. You have kept the good wine until now!"

¹¹This was the first powerful work Jesus did. It was done in Cana of Galilee where He showed His power. His followers put their trust in Him.

Kid-Builder Value
HELPFULNESS is service or assistance to someone else. Jesus showed helpfulness when He performed a miracle at a wedding.

KID-BUILDER Questions

- What did Jesus do to help at the wedding?
- How have people been helpful to you?
- Helping someone doesn't always mean performing a miracle. It could mean something as simple as doing a chore for a busy mother or helping a friend clean his room. What are some things you can do? How can you use your talents and abilities to help others?

KID-BUILDER Prayer

Lord, help me see the times when I can be helpful to others. Help me use what I have to serve You.

In Jesus' name. Amen.

Memory Verse:
O Lord God! . . . Nothing is too hard for You!   Jer. 32:17

● ●

JOHN

Nicodemus Asks Jesus about Life

John 3

There was a man named Nicodemus (NICK-uh-DEE-mus). He was a proud religious law-keeper and a leader of the Jews. ²He came to Jesus at night and said, "Teacher, we know You have come from God to teach us. No one can do these powerful works You do unless God is with Him."

³Jesus said to him, "For sure, I tell you, unless a man is born again, he cannot see the holy nation of God." ⁴Nicodemus said to Him, "How can a man be born when he is old? How can he get into his mother's body and be born the second time?" ⁵Jesus answered, "For sure, I tell you, unless a

Kid-Builder Fact
John 3:13 Son of Man was Jesus' favorite name for Himself. It is used seventy-eight times in the Gospels. With this term, Jesus identified Himself as a true man as well as being the Son of God. He often spoke of Himself this way when talking about the need to suffer and to give His life for the sins of all people.

man is born of water and of the Spirit of God, he cannot get into the holy nation of God. 6Whatever is born of the flesh is flesh. Whatever is born of the Spirit is spirit.

7"Do not be surprised that I said to you, 'You must be born again.' 8The wind blows where it wants to and you hear its sound. You do not know where it comes from or where it goes. It is the same with everyone who is born of the Spirit of God."

9Nicodemus said to Him, "How can this be?" 10Jesus said, "Are you a teacher among the Jews and do not know these things? 11For sure, I tell you, We are talking about things We know. We tell of what We have seen. Yet you do not take Our words to be true. 12I tell you about things of the earth and you do not believe them. How will you believe if I tell you things about heaven?

13"No one has gone up into heaven except the One Who came down from heaven. That One is the Son of Man Who is in heaven. 14As Moses lifted up the snake in the desert, so the Son of Man must be lifted up. 15Then whoever puts his trust in

Kid-Builder Fact
John 3:16 This "life that lasts forever" means life under God's saving rule. It comes from God through Jesus Christ. It begins when we accept Jesus Christ as Savior and seek to do the things that please Him instead of the things that please ourselves.

Him will have life that lasts forever. ¹⁶For God so loved the world that He gave His only Son. Whoever puts his trust in God's Son will not be lost but will have life that lasts forever. ¹⁷For God did not send His Son into the world to say it is guilty. He sent His Son so the world might be saved from the punishment of sin by Him. ¹⁸Whoever puts his trust in His Son is not guilty. Whoever does not put his trust in Him is guilty already. It is because he does not put his trust in the name of the only Son of God."

Kid-Builder Value
INITIATIVE (I-NISH-ah-tive) is the readiness to take needed action without waiting around for someone else to act. Nicodemus showed initiative when he went to talk to Jesus.

KID-BUILDER Questions

- What did Jesus tell Nicodemus about being born again?

- Nicodemus took Jesus' words to heart. Scripture later tells how he became a follower of Jesus. What could you do to find out more about Jesus?

- Read verse 16 again. This is God's promise to you. Have you asked Jesus to be your Savior?

KID-BUILDER Prayer

Lord, sometimes I have questions about Jesus like Nicodemus did. I want to find out more about Jesus. Thank You for sending the Holy Spirit and other Christians to help me find answers. Thank You for Your Word.   In Jesus' name. Amen.

Memory Verse:
For God so loved the world that He gave His only Son. Whoever puts his trust in God's Son will not be lost but will have life that lasts forever.   John 3:16

JOHN

Jesus Feeds Over 5,000 People

John 6

Jesus went over to the other side of the sea of Galilee. It is sometimes called Tiberias (ti-BIR-ee-ahs). 2Many people followed Him. They saw the powerful works He did on those who were sick. 3Jesus went up on a mountain and sat down with His followers. . . .

5Jesus looked up and saw many people coming to Him. He said to Philip, "Where can we buy bread to feed these people?" 6He said this to see what Philip would say. Jesus knew what He would do. 7Philip said to Him, "The money we have is not enough to buy bread to give each one a little."

8One of His followers was Andrew, Simon Peter's brother. He said to Jesus, 9"There is a boy here who has five loaves of barley bread and two small

Kid-Builder Fact
John 6:9 Barley was the most common grain grown in Israel. Most of the poor people used it for bread and cereal because it cost less than wheat.

fish. What is that for so many people?" [10]Jesus said, "Have the people sit down." There was much grass in that place. About five thousand men sat down.

[11]Jesus took the loaves and gave thanks. Then He gave the bread to those who were sitting down. The fish were given out the same way. The people had as much as they wanted. [12]When they were filled, Jesus said to His followers, "Gather up the pieces that are left. None will be wasted." [13]The followers gathered the pieces together. Twelve baskets were filled with pieces of barley bread. These were left after all the people had eaten.

[14]The people saw the powerful work Jesus had done. They said, "It is true! This is the One Who speaks for God Who is to come into the world."

Kid-Builder Value
UNSELFISHNESS is the ability to give of oneself out of concern for others. The boy who gave his lunch was unselfish. He had no promise of any lunch for himself. Yet, he gave it freely.

KID-BUILDER Questions

- In Jesus' time, there were no grocery stores or convenient drive-up restaurants. Feeding the people was a real need. Did Jesus' disciples believe that He could give the people food? Why?

- What do you have that you can use to help others?

- What is something you could give besides money or other objects?

KID-BUILDER Prayer

Thank You, God, for providing for my needs each day. Teach me to be unselfish. Help me use what I have to help others.   In Jesus' name. Amen.

Memory Verse:
Give, and it will be given to you. . . . The way you give to others is the way you will receive in return.   Luke 6:38

JOHN

Jesus Heals a Man Born Blind

John 9

As Jesus went on His way [from the temple], He saw a man who had been born blind. ²His followers asked Him, "Teacher, whose sin made this man to be born blind? Was it the sin of this man or the sin of his parents?" ³Jesus answered, "The sin of this man or the sin of his parents did not make him to be born blind. He was born blind so the work of God would be seen in him. . . ."

⁶After Jesus had said this, He spit on the ground. He mixed it with dust and put that mud on the eyes of the blind man. ⁷Then Jesus said to him, "Go and wash in the pool of Siloam." (Siloam means Sent.) The man went away and washed. When he came back, he could see.

⁸Neighbors and others had seen him begging.

Kid-Builder Fact
John 9:8 Beggars asked others for food or money. Many people in Bible times never had jobs. They lived from what others gave them. Beggars were often crippled or blind, and thus could not work.

They said, "Is not this the man who sat and begged?" 9Some said, "This is the one." Others said, "No, but he looks like him." But the man who had been blind said, "I am the man." 10They said to him, "How were your eyes opened?" 11He answered, "A Man called Jesus made mud and put it on my eyes. Then He said to me, 'Go and wash in the pool of Siloam.' I went and washed and I can see." 12Then they asked him, "Where is He?" He answered, "I do not know."

13They took the man who had been born blind to the proud religious law-keepers. 14It was the Day of Rest when Jesus had made mud and opened his eyes. 15Again the proud religious law-keepers asked the man who had been born blind how he had been made to see. He answered them, "Jesus put mud on my eyes. I washed and now I see!" 16Some of the proud religious law-keepers said, "The Man Who did this is not from God because He worked on the Day of Rest." Others said, "How can a sinful man do powerful works?" . . . 17They spoke again to the blind man, saying, "What do you say about Him since He opened your eyes?" He answered, "He is One Who speaks for God."

Kid-Builder Value
FAIRNESS is the ability to show honesty and impartiality. It might seem that God was unfair to allow the man to be blind for so many years. However, the man was used by God to show the world His great power. Miracles such as this one give us hope to believe God can take care of our needs today.

KID-BUILDER Questions

- What did Jesus do to help the blind man?

- Can you think of a situation at school or at home that didn't seem fair to you? How did you respond to the teacher or parent?

- Do you think it's possible to always be fair in every situation? Why?

KID-BUILDER Prayer

Lord, help me to trust You for the answers to questions I don't understand. Thank You for providing people like my mom and dad or my pastor to help me when circumstances don't seem fair. In Jesus' name. Amen.

Memory Verse:
Happy is he whose help is the God of Jacob, and whose hope is in the Lord his God. Ps. 146:5

JOHN

Jesus Brings Lazarus Back to Life

John 11

A man named Lazarus was sick. He lived in the town of Bethany with his sisters, Mary and Martha. . . . ³The sisters sent word to Jesus, saying, "Lord, your friend is sick!" ⁴When Jesus heard this, He said, "This sickness will not end in death. It has happened so that it will bring honor to God. And the Son of God will be honored by it also."

⁵Jesus loved Martha and her sister and Lazarus. ⁶But when He heard that Lazarus was sick, He stayed where He was two more days. . . . ¹¹Jesus . . . said, "Our friend Lazarus is sleeping. I will go and wake him up." ¹²The followers said to Him, "If he is sleeping, he will get well." ¹³But Jesus meant Lazarus was dead. They thought He meant Lazarus was resting in sleep. ¹⁴Then Jesus said to them, "Lazarus is dead. ¹⁵Because of you I am glad I was not there so that you may believe. Come, let us go to him." . . .

¹⁷When Jesus got there, He heard that Lazarus had been in the grave four days. ¹⁸Bethany was about one-half hour walk from Jerusalem. ¹⁹Many

Jews had come to Martha and Mary to give words of comfort about their brother.

²⁰Martha heard that Jesus was coming and went to meet Him. Mary stayed in the house. ²¹Martha said to Jesus, "Lord, if You had been here, my brother would not have died. ²²I know even now God will give You whatever You ask." ²³Jesus said to her, "Your brother will rise again." . . .

³²Mary went to the place where Jesus was. When she saw Him, she got down at His feet. She said to Him, "Lord, if You had been here, my brother would not have died." ³³Jesus saw her crying. The Jews who came with her were crying also. His heart was very sad and He was troubled. ³⁴He said, "Where did you lay Lazarus?" They said, "Lord,

Kid-Builder Fact
John 11:44 Grave clothes were the strips of linen cloth that were wrapped around a body before burial. Hands and feet were tied with more pieces of linen, and another piece was placed over the face.

come and see." [35]Then Jesus cried. [36]The Jews said, "See how much He loved Lazarus." [37]Some of them said, "This Man opened the eyes of the blind man. Could He not have kept this man from dying?"

[38]Jesus went to the grave with a sad heart. The grave was a hole in the side of a hill. A stone covered the door. [39]Jesus said, "Take the stone away."

The dead man's sister, Martha, said to Him, "Lord by now his body has a bad smell. He has been dead four days." 40Jesus said to her, "Did I not say that if you would believe, you would see the shining greatness of God?"

41They took the stone away. Jesus looked up and said, "Father, I thank You for hearing Me. 42I know You always hear Me. But I have said this for the people standing here, so they may believe You have sent Me."

43When He had said this, He called with a loud voice, "Lazarus, come out!" 44The man who had been dead came out. His hands and feet were tied in grave clothes. A white cloth was tied around his face. Jesus said to the people, "Take off the grave clothes and let him go!"

Kid-Builder Value
CONCERN is a feeling of anxiety, or interest in, someone else. Jesus showed concern when He grieved with Mary and Martha.

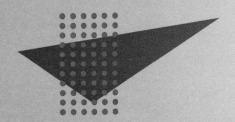

KID-BUILDER Questions

- How did Jesus show concern for Mary and Martha?
- Mary and Martha were scared and hurt about their brother. Have you ever felt that way? How did someone show concern for you?
- How do you show concern for others?

KID-BUILDER Prayer

Thank You, God, for the people who take care of me each day.   *In Jesus' name. Amen.*

Memory Verse:
Give all your worries to Him because He cares for you.   I Pet. 5:7

JOHN

The Last Supper

John 13

Jesus knew the time had come for Him to leave this world and go to the Father. He had loved His own who were in the world. He loved them to the end. ²He and His followers were having supper. Satan had put the thought into the heart of Judas Iscariot of handing Jesus over to the leaders of the country. ³Jesus knew the Father had put everything into His hands. He knew He had come from God and was going back to God. ⁴Jesus got up from the supper and took off His coat. He picked up a cloth and put it around Him. ⁵Then He put water into a wash pan and began to wash the feet of His followers. He dried their feet with the cloth He had put around Himself.

⁶Jesus came to Simon Peter. Peter said to Him, "Lord, are You going to wash my feet?" ⁷Jesus answered him, "You do not understand now what I am doing but you will later." ⁸Peter said to him, "I will never let You wash my feet." Jesus said, "Unless I wash you, you will not be a part of Me."

Kid-Builder Fact
John 13:5 Foot washing was a special way to greet guests
after they traveled. People traveled mainly by walking on the
hot, dusty roads of Israel. After a long journey, their feet would
be tired and dirty. Servants would use a bowl of cool water
and fresh towels to bathe the feet of the travelers.

[9]Simon Peter said to Him, "Lord, do not wash only my feet, but wash my hands and my head also." [10]Jesus said to him, "Anyone who has washed his body needs only to wash his feet. Then he is clean all over. You are all clean except one." Jesus knew who was going to hand Him over to the leaders. That is why He said, "You are all clean except one."

... [31]After Judas went out, Jesus said, "The Son of Man is now honored and God has been honored in Him. [32]If God is honored in Him, God will also honor Him in Himself right now. [33]Little children, I will be with you only a little while. You will look for Me. I say to you what I said to the Jews, 'Where I am going, you cannot come!' [34]I give you a new Law. You are to love each other. You must love each other as I have loved you. [35]If you love each other, all men will know you are My followers."

Kid-Builder Value
HUMILITY is the voluntary lowering of yourself or the willingness to give up something that should rightfully be yours. Jesus showed humility and love when He washed His followers' feet. Through His example, they were to love each other as well.

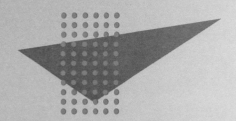

KID-BUILDER Questions

- How did Jesus show humility?

- Suppose the president came to your house and offered to clean your cat's litter box or some other chore you normally do. How would you feel? Would you have the same reaction as Peter?

- What are some ways you can put others first?

KID-BUILDER Prayer

Lord, I want to follow Jesus' example. But sometimes I don't know how. Please help me know what to do.
In Jesus' name. Amen.

Memory Verse:
Be kind to others and have no pride. Be gentle and be willing to wait
for others.   Col. 3:12b

JOHN

Jesus Is Raised from the Grave

John 20

It was the first day of the week. Mary Magdalene came to the grave early in the morning while it was still dark. She saw that the stone had been pushed away from the grave. ²She ran to Simon Peter and the other follower whom Jesus loved. She said to them, "They have taken the Lord out of the grave. We do not know where they have put Him."

³Then Peter and the other follower went to the grave. ⁴They ran but the other follower ran faster than Peter and came to the grave first. ⁵He got down and looked in and saw the linen cloths but did not go in. ⁶Then Simon Peter came and went into the grave. He saw the linen cloths lying there. ⁷The white cloth that had been around the head of Jesus was not lying with the other linen cloths. It was rolled up and lying apart by itself. ⁸Then the other follower, who had come first, went in also. He saw and believed. . . .

¹¹Mary stood outside the grave crying. As she

cried, she got down and looked inside the grave. [12]She saw two angels dressed in white clothes. They were sitting where the body of Jesus had lain. One angel was where His head had lain and one angel was where His feet had lain. [13]They said to her, "Woman, why are you crying?" She said to them, "Because they have taken away my Lord. I do not know where they have put Him."

[14]After saying this, she turned around and saw Jesus standing there. But she did not know that it was Jesus. [15]He said to her, "Woman, why are you crying? Who are you looking for?" She thought He was the man who cared for the garden. She said to Him, "Sir, if you have taken Jesus from here, tell me where you have put Him. I will take Him away." [16]Jesus said to her, "Mary!" She turned around and said to Him, "Teacher!" [17]Jesus said to her, "Do not hold on to Me. I have not yet gone up to My Father. But go to My brothers. Tell them I will go up to My Father and your Father, and to My God and your God!" [18]Mary Magdalene went and told the followers that she had seen the Lord. She told them the things He had said to her.

[19]It was evening of the first day of the week. The followers had gathered together with the doors locked because they were afraid of the Jews. Jesus came and stood among them. He said, "May you have peace." [20]When He had said this, He showed them His hands and His side. When the followers

saw the Lord, they were filled with joy. . . .

24Thomas was not with them when Jesus came. . . . 25The other followers told him, "We have seen the Lord!" He said to them, "I will not believe until I see the marks made by the nails in His hands. I will not believe until I put my finger into the marks of the nails. I will not believe until I put my hand into His side."

26Eight days later the followers were again inside a house. Thomas was with them. The doors were locked. Jesus came and stood among them. He said, "May you have peace!" 27He said to Thomas, "Put your finger into My hands. Put your hand into My side. Do not doubt, believe!" 28Thomas said to Him, "My Lord and my God!" 29Jesus said to him, "Thomas, because you have seen Me, you believe. Those are happy who have never seen Me and yet believe!"

30Jesus did many other powerful works in front of His followers. They are not written in this book. 31But these are written so you may believe that Jesus is the Christ, the Son of God. When you put your trust in Him, you will have life that lasts forever through His name.

Kid-Builder Value
FAITH is the act of believing the things that God has revealed about Himself, and acting on those beliefs. Jesus' resurrection gave His followers faith to serve Him.

KID-BUILDER Questions

- How did Jesus help Thomas not to doubt?

- Have you ever heard news that sounded almost too good to be true? How did you go about finding out whether it was true?

- Jesus did not get mad at Thomas because he had doubts. Instead, Jesus helped Thomas believe in Him. How can this truth help you when you have doubts?

KID-BUILDER Prayer

Lord, when I have doubts, it's nice to know I can talk to You about them. Thank You, Lord, for helping me find answers.   *In Jesus' name. Amen.*

Memory Verse:
These are written so you may believe that Jesus is the Christ, the Son of God. When you put your trust in Him, you will have life that lasts forever through His name.   John 20:31

JOHN

Jesus Appears to His Followers

John 21

Jesus ... showed Himself to His followers at the lake of Tiberias. It happened like this: ²Simon Peter and Thomas who was called the Twin and Nathanael from the town of Cana in the country of Galilee and the sons of Zebedee and two other followers were all together. ³Simon Peter said to them, "I am going fishing." The others said, "We will go with you." They went out and got into a boat. That night they caught no fish.

⁴Early in the morning Jesus stood on the shore of the lake. The followers did not know it was Jesus. ⁵Then Jesus said to them, "Children, do you have any fish?" They said, "No." ⁶He said to them, "Put your net over the right side of the boat. Then you will catch some fish." They put out the net.

Kid-Builder Fact
John 21:3 Some of Jesus' followers were fishermen. Fishermen worked along every lake, river, or sea to catch fish. They fished mostly with large nets but also with hooks and spears. Fishing at night was common on the Sea of Galilee.

309

They were not able to pull it in because it was so full of fish.

⁷Then the follower whom Jesus loved said to Peter, "It is the Lord!" When Peter heard it was the Lord, he put on his fisherman's coat. (He had taken it off.) Then he jumped into

the water. ⁸The other followers came in the boat. They were pulling the net with the fish. They were not far from land, only a little way out.

⁹When they came to land they saw fish and bread on a fire. ¹⁰Jesus said to them, "Bring some of the fish you have just caught." ¹¹Simon Peter went out and pulled the net to land. There were 153 big fish. The net was not broken even with so many. . . .

¹⁵When they were finished eating, Jesus said to Simon Peter, "Simon, son of John, do you love Me more than these?" Peter answered Jesus, "Yes, Lord, You know that I love You." Jesus said to him, "Feed My lambs."

¹⁶Jesus said to Peter the second time, "Simon, son of John, do you love Me?" He answered Jesus, "Yes, Lord, You know that I love You." Jesus said to him, "Take care of My sheep."

¹⁷Jesus said to Peter the third time, "Simon, son of John, do you love Me?" Peter felt bad because Jesus asked him the third time, "Do you love Me?" He answered Jesus, "Lord, You know everything. You know I love You." Jesus said to him, "Feed My sheep."

Kid-Builder Value
FORGIVENESS refers to blotting out sin and guilt. Jesus showed forgiveness when He forgave Peter and gave Him a brand-new start.

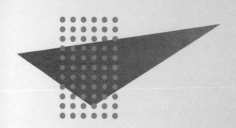

KID-BUILDER Questions

- How many times did Peter deny Jesus? (See Matt. 26:69-75.) How many times did Jesus ask Peter if he loved Him?

- Is there someone you need to forgive? How can you show forgiveness?

- Have you ever hoped for something so much that when it happened you almost didn't believe it? Jesus' followers felt that way when they saw Jesus alive. Forgiveness does that too. Read the verse at the bottom of this page. This is a promise from God. Have you asked God to forgive you?

KID-BUILDER Prayer

Thank You, God, for forgiving me when I've blown it. Help me to do the same thing when others fail me.
In Jesus' name. Amen.

Memory Verse:
If we tell Him our sins, He is faithful and we can depend on Him to forgive us of our sins. He will make our lives clean from all sin.
I John 1:9

Church History

The fifth book of the New Testament is the *Acts of the Apostles*. It tells us about the history of the early church. It was written by the doctor Luke after he wrote the Gospel of Luke.

Acts of the Apostles

With the exception of the first chapter, the action of the Book of *Acts* takes place several years after Jesus returned to heaven. It tells us how the Christian church began with a small group of praying believers in Jerusalem on the Day of Pentecost. When the Holy Spirit came on them, they wanted to tell others the good news, and the church grew and spread across the Roman Empire. *Acts* also tells us the stories of Peter, Paul, and other Christians and their work for the Lord. Many of the stories you may have heard about—Paul's conversion on the Damascus Road, Peter's release from prison, the healing of the crippled beggar, and the missionary journeys of Paul—are all found in the pages of *Acts*.

ACTS

Pentecost—The Birth of the Church

Acts 1—2

Before Jesus left to return to heaven, He told His followers of a special promise.

As they were gathered together with Him, He told them, "Do not leave Jerusalem. Wait for what the Father has promised. You heard Me speak of this. ⁵For John the Baptist baptized with water but in a few days you will be baptized with the Holy Spirit." . . .

²:¹The followers of Jesus were all together in one place fifty days after the special religious gathering to remember how the Jews left Egypt. ²All at once there was a sound from heaven like a powerful wind. It filled the house where they were sitting. ³Then they saw tongues which were divided that looked like fire. These came down on each one of them. ⁴They were all filled with the Holy Spirit. Then they began to speak in other languages which the Holy Spirit made them able to speak.

⁵There were many religious Jews staying in Jerusalem. They were from every country of the

world. 6When they heard this strange sound, they gathered together. They all listened! It was hard for them to believe they were hearing words in their own language. 7They were surprised and wondered about it. They said to each other, "Are not these Galileans who are speaking? 8How is it that each one of us can hear his own language? . . ." 12They were all surprised and wondered about this. They said to each other, "What can this mean?" 13But others laughed and made fun, saying, "These men are full of new wine."

14Then Peter stood up with the eleven missionaries and spoke with a loud voice, . . . 15"These men are not drunk as you think. It is only nine o'clock in the morning. 16The early preacher Joel said this would happen. 17God says, 'In the last days I will send My Spirit on all men. Then your sons and daughters will speak God's Word.' . . .

22"Jewish men, listen to what I have to say! You knew Jesus of the town of Nazareth by the powerful works He did. God worked through Jesus while He was with you. You all know this. . . . 23You had sinful men take Him and nail Him to a cross. 24But God raised Him up. . . .

Kid-Builder Fact
Acts 2:14 The word *missionary*, or *apostle* refers to the twelve men chosen by Jesus as His special followers. It means *one chosen and sent*. Paul was not one of the twelve followers, but he was known as an *apostle*.

Death could not hold its power over Him. . . .

³²"Jesus is this One! God has raised Him up and we have all seen Him.

³³"This Jesus has been lifted up to God's right side. The Holy Spirit was promised by the Father. God has given Him to us. That is what you are seeing and hearing now!" . . .

³⁷When the Jews heard this, their hearts were troubled. They said to Peter and to the other missionaries, "Brothers, what should we do?" ³⁸Peter said to them, "Be sorry for your sins and turn from them and be baptized in the name of Jesus Christ,

and your sins will be forgiven. You will receive the gift of the Holy Spirit. 39This promise is to you and your children. It is to all people everywhere. It is to as many as the Lord our God will call.". . . 41Those who believed what he said were baptized. There were about 3000 more followers added that day.

42They were faithful in listening to the teaching of the missionaries. They worshiped and prayed and ate the Lord's supper together. 43Many powerful works were done by the missionaries. . . . 44All those who put their trust in Christ were together and shared what they owned. 45As anyone had need, they sold what they owned and shared with everyone. 46Day after day they went to the house of God together. In their houses they ate their food together. Their hearts were happy. . . . 47The Lord added to the group each day those who were being saved from the punishment of sin.

Kid-Builder Value
FELLOWSHIP is what happens when two or more people with similar interests or feelings get together. Christians experience fellowship in a special way because their common interest is Jesus. When the early Christians received the Holy Spirit, they showed their newfound love by sharing what they had with one another.

KID-BUILDER Questions

- What evidence pointed to the Holy Spirit's arrival?

- How did the people respond after hearing Peter speak?

- The Holy Spirit gave the followers of Jesus a new love for others. They expressed their love by sharing themselves and what they had with others. In what ways can you share with others?

- What does fellowship mean to you? In what ways do you fellowship with other people in your church? In what ways does your family fellowship with other families?

KID-BUILDER Prayer

Lord, thank You for sending the Holy Spirit. Guide me in Your truth, and show me opportunities where I can share Your love with others.

In Jesus' name. Amen.

Memory Verse:
Let us help each other to love others and to do good.   Heb. 10:24

ACTS

Peter and John Help a Crippled Beggar

Acts 3

Peter and John were going to the house of God about three o'clock. It was the time for prayer. ²Each day a certain man was carried to the Beautiful Gate of the house of God. This man had never been able to walk. He was there begging for money from those who were going in. ³He asked Peter and John for money when he saw them going in. ⁴Peter and John looked at him. Then Peter said, "Look at us" ⁵The man who could not walk looked at them. He thought he would get something from them. ⁶Peter said, "I have no money, but what I have I will give you! In the name of Jesus Christ of Nazareth, get up and walk!" ⁷Peter took the man by the right hand and lifted

Kid-Builder Value
FAITH is the act of believing the things that God has revealed about Himself and acting on those beliefs. Peter and John's faith in God resulted in a miraculous healing for a crippled beggar.

him up. At once his feet and the bones in his legs became strong. ⁸He jumped up on his feet and walked. Then he went into the house of God with them. He gave thanks to God as he walked.

⁹All the people saw him walking and giving thanks to God. ¹⁰They knew it was the man who had been sitting and begging at the Beautiful Gate. They were surprised he was walking. ¹¹The man who was healed held on to Peter and John. All the people who were surprised gathered together around them in a place called Solomon's Porch.

KID-BUILDER Questions

- What did the man want from Peter and John? What did Peter and John do for him instead?

- Did Peter have faith in his own ability to heal the man? How do you know?

- Does having faith mean that God will grant us everything we want when we want it? Why or why not?

KID-BUILDER Prayer

Lord, sometimes I don't know how to trust You. For those times, help me have faith in You.

In Jesus' name. Amen.

Memory Verse:
The one who has faith can do all things.   Mark 9:23b

ACTS

Paul Is Converted

Acts 9

Paul, one of the greatest missionaries ever, was not always a believer. Known as Saul of Tarsus, he was a member of the Sanhedrin—the ruling council of the Jewish people. Paul had authority to put believers to death.

Saul was still talking much about how he would like to kill the followers of the Lord. He went to the head religious leader. ²He asked for letters to be written to the Jewish places of worship in the city of Damascus. The letters were to say that if he found any men or women following the Way of Christ he might bring them to Jerusalem in chains.

³He went on his way until he came near Damascus. All at once he saw a light from heaven shining around him. ⁴He fell to the ground. Then he heard a voice say, "Saul, Saul, why are you working so hard against Me?"

⁵Saul answered, "Who are You, Lord?" He said, "I am Jesus, the One Whom you are working

against. You hurt yourself by trying to hurt Me." 6Saul was shaken and surprised. Then he said, "What do you want me to do, Lord?" The Lord said to him, "Get up! Go into the city and you will be told what to do."

7Those with Saul were not able to say anything. They heard a voice but saw no one. 8Saul got up from the ground. When he opened his eyes, he saw nothing. They took him by the hand and led him to Damascus. 9He could not see for three days. During that time he did not eat or drink.

10In Damascus there was a follower by the name of Ananias. The Lord showed him in a dream what He wanted him to see. He said, "Ananias!" And Ananias answered, "Yes, Lord, I am here." 11The Lord said, "Get up! Go over to Straight Street to Judas' house and ask for a man from the city of Tarsus. His name is Saul. You will find him praying there. 12Saul has seen a man called Ananias in a dream. He is to come and put his hands on Saul so he might see again."

13Ananias said, "But Lord, many people have told me about this man. He is the reason many of Your followers in Jerusalem have had to suffer much. 14He came here with the right and the power from the head religious leaders to put everyone in

Kid-Builder Fact
Acts 9:2 The *Way of Christ* refers to believers in Jesus.

chains who call on Your name."  15The Lord said to him, "Go! This man is the one I have chosen to carry My name among the people who are not Jews and to their kings and to Jews. 16I will show him how much he will have to suffer because of Me."

17So Ananias went to that house. He put his hands on Saul and said, "Brother Saul, the Lord Jesus has sent me to you. You saw the Lord along the road as you came here. The Lord has sent me so you might be able to see again and be filled with the Holy Spirit." 18At once something like a covering fell from the eyes

of Saul and he could see. He got up and was baptized. ¹⁹After that he ate some food and received strength. For some days he stayed with the followers in Damascus.

²⁰At once Saul began to preach in the Jewish places of worship that Jesus is the Son of God. ²¹All who heard him were surprised. . . .

Kid-Builder Value
CONVICTION is a strong belief in or desire to uphold a moral standard. Your personal convictions are the things you hold to be right or wrong. They mold your thoughts and actions. Paul had conviction about the truth of Christ when he learned about Him on the road to Damascus. When we have a sense of conviction about what we do, we are able to complete our tasks.

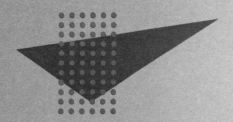

KID-BUILDER Questions

- What was Paul on his way to do?
- How was his mind changed about Jesus?
- Do you remember when you first learned of who Jesus is? What did you think about Him before that time?
- What do you strongly believe about God?

KID-BUILDER Prayer

Lord, help me live the truth that I believe about Jesus. In Jesus' name. Amen.

Memory Verse:
For the love of Christ puts us into action. We are sure that Christ died for everyone. So, because of that, everyone has a part in His death.   II Cor. 5:14

Peter Prays for Dorcas

Acts 9

A woman who was a follower lived in the city of Joppa. Her name was Tabitha, or Dorcas. She did many good things and many acts of kindness. ³⁷One day she became sick and died. After they had washed her body, they laid her in a room on the second floor. ³⁸The city of Lydda was near Joppa. The followers heard that Peter was at Lydda and sent two men to ask him to come at once. ³⁹Peter went back with them. When he came, they took him to the room. All the women whose husbands had died were standing around crying. They were showing the clothes Dorcas had made while she was with them.

⁴⁰Peter made them all leave the room. Then he got down on his knees and prayed. He turned to her body and said, "Tabitha, get up!" She opened her eyes and looked at Peter and sat up. ⁴¹He took her by the hand and lifted her up. Then he called in the faithful followers and the women whose husbands had died. He

gave her to them, a living person.

⁴²News of this went through all Joppa. Many people put their trust in the Lord. ⁴³After this, Peter stayed in Joppa many days in the house of Simon who worked with leather.

Kid-Builder Value
KINDNESS combines a sympathetic attitude with the willingness to be helpful whenever possible. Dorcas's kindness was known throughout the city of Joppa. Jesus wants us to be known as people of kindness.

KID-BUILDER Questions

- What are some of the kind things Dorcas did to help others?

- Dorcas's kindness was remembered by a lot of people. What would you like people to remember about you?

KID-BUILDER Prayer

Lord, help me be kind to others without looking for something in return.   *In Jesus' name. Amen.*

Memory Verse:
As you live God-like, be kind to Christian brothers and love them.

II Pet. 1:7

ACTS

Peter Is Arrested

Acts 12

At that time King Herod used his power to make it hard for the Christians in the church. 2He killed James, the brother of John, with a sword. 3When he saw that it made the Jews happy, he took hold of Peter also. This was during the special religious gathering to remember how the Jews left Egypt. 4Herod took Peter and put him in prison and had sixteen soldiers watch him. After the special religious gathering was over, he planned to bring Peter out to the people. . . .

5But the church kept praying to God for him. 6The night before Herod was to bring him out for his trial, Peter was sleeping between two soldiers. He was tied with two chains. Soldiers stood by the door and watched the prison.

7All at once an angel of the Lord was seen standing beside him. A light shone in the building. The angel hit Peter on the side and said, "Get up!" Then the chains fell off his hands. 8The angel said, "Put on your belt and shoes!" He did. The angel

said to Peter, "Put on your coat and follow me."
⁹Peter followed him out. He was not sure what was
happening as the angel helped him. He thought it
was a dream.

¹⁰They passed one soldier, then another one.
They came to the big iron door that leads to the
city and it opened by itself and they went through.

As soon as they had gone up one street, the angel left him.

¹¹As Peter began to see what was happening, he said to himself, "Now I am sure the Lord has sent His angel and has taken me out of the hands of Herod. . . ." ¹²After thinking about all this, he went to Mary's house. She was the mother of John Mark. Many Christians were gathered there praying.

¹³When Peter knocked at the gate, a girl named Rhoda went to see who it was. ¹⁴She knew Peter's voice, but in her joy she forgot to open the gate. She ran in and told them that Peter was standing outside the gate.

¹⁵They said to her, "You are crazy." But she said again that it was so. They kept saying, "It is his angel." ¹⁶Peter kept knocking. When they opened the gate and saw him, they were surprised and wondered about it. ¹⁷He raised his hand and told them not to talk but to listen to him. He told them how the Lord had brought him out of prison. He said, "Tell all these things to James and to the other Christian brothers." Then he went to another place.

Kid-Builder Value
PRAYERFULNESS is regular participation in prayer. The followers were prayerful when Peter was put in prison. The results were miraculous! God wants our lives to be filled with regular communication with Him.

KID-BUILDER Questions

- Why was Peter in prison? How did he get out of prison?

- Why do you think the people had a hard time believing that Peter had been set free, even though they had prayed for him to be released?

- Have there been times that you have prayed for something but did not really believe God would help you? Do you need faith to be prayerful? Why or why not?

KID-BUILDER Prayer

Lord, sometimes I have a hard time believing that You listen to my prayers. Help me continue in prayer even when I doubt. In Jesus' name. Amen.

Memory Verse:
The prayer from the heart of a man right with God has much power.
Jas. 5:16b

ACTS

Paul and Silas

Acts 16

Paul and Silas were on a missionary journey to preach the Gospel. But they were not always welcomed. Sometimes they suffered hard times.

One day as [Paul and Silas] were going to the place to pray, [they] met a servant-girl who could tell what was going to happen in the future by a demon she had. Her owner made much money from her power. ¹⁷She followed Paul . . . crying out, "These are servants of the Highest God. They are telling you how to be saved from the punishment of sin." ¹⁸She did this many days. Paul was troubled. Then he turned and said to the demon in her, "In the name of Jesus Christ, I speak to you. Come out of her!" At once it left her.

¹⁹The girl's owners saw that they could not make money with her anymore. Then they took hold of Paul and Silas and dragged them to the leaders. . . . ²⁰After they brought them in front of the leaders, they said, "These men are Jews and are making a lot of trouble in our city. ²¹They are teaching a reli-

gion that we Romans are not allowed to follow."

²²Many people had gathered around Paul and Silas. They were calling out things against them. The leaders had . . . Paul and Silas . . . beaten with sticks. ²³After they had hit them many times, they put Paul and Silas in prison. The soldiers told the man who watched the prison to be sure to keep them from getting away. ²⁴Because of this, they were put in the inside room of the prison and their feet were put in pieces of wood that held them.

²⁵About midnight Paul and Silas were praying and singing songs of thanks to God. The other men in prison were listening to them. ²⁶All at once the earth started to shake. The stones under the prison shook and the doors opened. The chains fell off from everyone.

²⁷The man who watched the prison woke up. He saw the prison doors wide open and thought the men in prison had gotten away. At once he pulled out his sword to kill himself. ²⁸But Paul called to him, "Do not hurt yourself. We are all here!" ²⁹The man who watched the prison called for a light. Then he ran in and got down in front of Paul and Silas. He was shaking with fear. ³⁰As he took them outside, he said, "Sirs, what must I do to be saved?"

Kid-Builder Value
JOYFULNESS is an intense feeling of good. Paul and Silas expressed joy, even though they were in prison.

³¹They said, "Put your trust in the Lord Jesus Christ and you and your family will be saved from the punishment of sin."

³²Then Paul spoke the Word of God to him and his family. ³³It was late at night, but the man who watched the prison took Paul and Silas in and washed the places on their bodies where they were hurt. Right then he and his family were baptized. ³⁴He took Paul and Silas to his house and gave them food. He and all his family were full of joy for having put their trust in God.

KID-BUILDER Questions

- Why were Paul and Silas put in prison? Was that fair or unfair?

- How did they share their joy with the jailer?

- Was there a time when you felt joyful, even though you were in the middle of a hard situation? What happened?

KID-BUILDER Prayer

Lord, help me focus on the joy You give me, rather than looking only to my circumstances.

In Jesus' name. Amen.

Memory Verse:
But let those who are right and good be glad. Let them be happy before God. Yes, let them be full of joy.　　　Ps. 68:3

ACTS

Trouble at Sea

Acts 27

Paul had been arrested and jailed many times for preaching the Gospel. When he was arrested and put on trial, he asked to be sent to Rome to be tried before the Roman emperor.

It was decided that we should go to the country of Italy by ship. Then they put Paul and some other men in chains. Julius, a captain of Caesar's army, was to watch them. ²We went on a ship that . . . was going to stop at the towns along the seashore of Asia. . . . ³The next day we stopped in the city of Sidon. Julius was kind to Paul. He let him visit friends who cared for him.

⁴After leaving Sidon we were blown by the wind along the south side of the island of Cyprus. . . . ⁸The wind was against us, and we did not sail very fast. Then we came to a place called Fair Havens. . . .

⁹Much time had been lost. To keep going that late in the year would mean danger. Paul spoke with strong words, ¹⁰"Sirs, it looks to me as if this

ship and its freight will be lost. We are in danger of being lost also."

11The captain of the soldiers listened to what the captain of the ship said and not to what Paul said. . . . 12Most of those on the ship wanted to go on and try to get to Phoenix. . . .

13When a south wind started to blow, they thought their plan was right. They pulled up the anchor and went close to the shore of Crete.

14Later a bad wind storm came down from the land. It was called a northeaster. . . . 18The storm was so bad the high waves were beating against the ship. The next day the men threw some of the freight over into the sea. 19On the third day, with their own hands, they threw part of the sails and ropes into the sea. 20We did not see the sun or stars for many days. A very bad storm kept beating against us. We lost all hope of being saved.

21No one had eaten for a long time. Then Paul stood up and said to them, "Men, you should have listened to me and not left Crete. You would not have had this trouble and loss. 22But now I want you to take hope. No one will lose his life. Only the ship will be lost. 23I belong to God and I work for Him. Last night an angel of God stood by me 24and

Kid-Builder Value
COURAGE is the ability and willingness to stand firm when confronted by danger, fear, or peer pressure. Paul had courage when faced with being shipwrecked.

said, 'Do not be afraid, Paul. You must stand in front of Caesar. God has given you the lives of all the men on this ship.' 25So take hope, men. I believe my God will do what He has told me. 26 But the ship will be lost on some island."

27It was now the fourteenth night. We were going with the wind on the Adriatic Sea. At midnight the sailors thought land was near. . . .

39In the morning . . . [t]hey planned to run the ship onto the sand if they could. 40The anchors were cut loose and left in the sea. . . . When they put up the sail, the wind took the ship toward shore. 41But the ship hit a place where the water was low. . . . The front of the ship did not move but the back part broke in pieces by the high waves.

42The soldiers planned to kill the men in chains. They were afraid they would swim to shore and get away, 43but the captain wanted to save Paul. He kept them from their plan. Calling out to those who could swim, he told them to jump into the sea and swim to shore. 44The others should use wood or anything from the ship. In this way, they all got to shore without getting hurt.

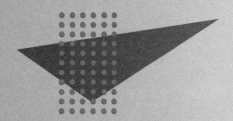

KID-BUILDER Questions

- What trouble at sea did Paul predict?
- Did anyone believe him? What did the sailors do?
- How did Paul's prediction come true?
- This was a life-and-death situation for Paul. What are some everyday situations you face that require courage?

KID-BUILDER Prayer

Lord, I need courage to face _____ (fill in a situation you are facing). Help me be strong and not fearful.   *In Jesus' name. Amen.*

Memory Verse:
We are pressed on every side, but we still have room to move. We are often in much trouble, but we never give up. People make it very hard for us, but we are not left alone. We are knocked down, but we are not destroyed.   II Cor. 4:8, 9

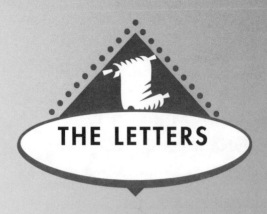

THE LETTERS

The Letters

There are twenty-one letters in the New Testament. Some people call them epistles. They were written mostly to specific churches, but some were written to Christians everywhere. *The Letters* explain important truths of the Christian faith, help deal with specific problems, encourage Christians, teach them, or correct false ideas. Thirteen were written by the apostle Paul; others were written by James, John, Peter, and Jude. We do not know the author of Hebrews.

The following is a list of the letters in the order in which they appear in the Bible:

Romans

Written by Paul to Christians in Rome, *Romans* (ROW-munz) was written to help believers learn more about God. Many Scriptures in this book point to Christ as the way of salvation.

I and II Corinthians

The apostle Paul wrote two letters to the church at Corinth, in what is now southern Greece. He wrote them during his third missionary journey. In *I Corinthians* (KORE-in-thee-enz), Paul answered questions the Christians in Corinth were having regarding problems in their church. He reminded them that Christ alone was their Master and everything should be used to glorify God. In his second letter, Paul shares some of his personal experiences and hardships.

Galatians

Paul wrote to the churches in southern Galatia—churches Paul helped to start on his first missionary journey. The church in Galatia was having trouble with Jewish Christians who felt that new Christians should not only believe in Jesus, but follow the old Jewish rituals as well. Paul wrote *Galatians* (guh-LAY-shuns) to set them straight.

Ephesians

Paul was under house arrest in Rome when he wrote to the church at Ephesus. He wanted to encourage the Ephesian (ee-FEE-shun) Christians by telling them that God does not have favorites—He loves everyone the same. God's children are special to Him, and He will give them the strength to say no to temptation.

Philippians

Even though Paul writes this letter from prison, he encourages the Philippian (fuh-LIP-ee-un) church to have joy in all circumstances and to think about things that are true, pure, lovely, and respected.

Colossians

Paul wrote this letter to the church in Colosse, a city in the southwestern part of what is now called Turkey. He warned the church against worshiping angels and against false teachers. He tells the Colossians (kuh-LAH-shuns) that God is ruler over all things, and He is in control of everything.

I and II Thessalonians

Paul writes to the church at Thessalonica—a church he started during his second missionary journey. In *I* and *II Thessalonians* (thess-uh-LOW-nee-uns), Paul encourages the believers to look for Jesus' second coming, when He comes for those who believe in Him. Meanwhile, Paul reminds them that the best way to prepare for the Lord's return is to live each day in a way that pleases Him.

I and II Timothy

First and *II Timothy* (TIM-uh-thee) are two letters Paul wrote to Timothy, a young pastor of the church at Ephesus. Timothy helped Paul spread the Gospel on some of his missionary journeys. Paul called Timothy his "son in the Christian faith" (I Tim. 1:2). The first letter to Timothy was written before Paul's imprisonment in Rome. The second letter was Paul's last letter before he was executed in Rome. Paul gave Timothy guidelines for leadership—guidelines that are useful for situations believers face today.

Titus

Titus (TIE-tus) is a letter from Paul to his friend Titus, a pastor on the island of Crete. Paul encourages Titus to become a good leader, obey the government, keep out of arguments, and be ready to do good deeds.

Philemon

This letter was written to persuade Philemon (feye-LEE-mun), a Christian man in Colosse, to forgive Onesimus (oh-NESS-ih-muss), a runaway slave. Onesimus had stolen from Philemon and run away to Rome, where he met Paul and became a Christian. Paul sent Onesimus back with this letter.

Hebrews

Hebrews (HEE-brooz) is a letter to Jewish Christians explaining who Jesus is and His connection with the Old Testament. No one knows for sure who the author is, but he did know the Old Testament. He wanted readers to know that Jesus is "greater and better than the angels" (Heb. 1:4) and "is as God is in every way" (Heb. 1:3).

James

The Book of *James* was written by James, the brother of Jesus. It tells believers that they must do more than talk about their faith. They must do what is pleasing to God—pray for friends and family, resist temptation, seek wisdom from God, and realize that everything they have comes from God.

I and II Peter

The letters of *I* and *II Peter* were directed to the Christians in northern Asia Minor (now Turkey). Peter wrote to encourage the Christians to have joy and trust God even though they would be facing persecution. He also warned them about listening to false teachers.

I, II, and III John

The apostle John, who is known as the Apostle of Love, wrote three letters—*I, II,* and *III John.* The first letter is to a church (Asia Minor); the second is to a Christian woman and her children; and the third is to Gaius, Paul's friend. He warns them about false teachers who would attempt to lead Christians away from Christ. He encouraged the believers to love God and treat their family and friends with love because God Himself is love. He encourages them to know and obey the Bible and show hospitality to others.

Jude

Jude is written by one of the half brothers of Jesus. In this letter, Jude warns believers to look out for those who say it was all right to do bad things and live as you please. He condemns complainers, people who brag about themselves, and are sinful. He says Christians must stay close to Christ and obey Him.

ROMANS

God Loves Us

Romans 8

We know that God makes all things work together for the good of those who love Him and are chosen to be a part of His plan. 29God knew from the beginning who would put their trust in Him. So He chose them and made them to be like His Son. Christ was first and all those who belong to God are His brothers. 30He called to Himself also those He chose. Those He called, He made right with Himself. Then He shared His shining greatness with those He made right with Himself.

31What can we say about all these things? Since God is for us, who can be against us? 32God did not keep His own Son for Himself but gave Him for us all. Then with His Son, will He not give us all things? 33Who can say anything against the people God has chosen? It is God Who says they are right with Himself. 34Who then can say we are guilty? It was Christ Jesus Who died. He was raised from the dead. He is on the right side of God praying to

Him for us. 35Who can keep us away from the love of Christ? Can trouble or problems? Can suffering wrong from others or no food? Can it be because of no clothes or because of danger or war? . . . 37But we have power over all these things through Jesus Who loves us so much. 38For I know that nothing can keep us from the love of God. Death cannot! Life cannot! Angels cannot! Leaders cannot! Any other power cannot! Hard things now or in the future cannot! 39The world above or the world below cannot! Any other living thing cannot keep us away from the love of God which is ours through Christ Jesus our Lord.

Kid-Builder Value
CONFIDENCE is a feeling of security based on faith and trust. Knowing that the love of Jesus is an unchanging fact in our lives can help us feel confident.

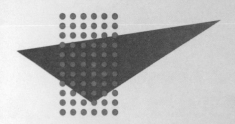

KID-BUILDER Questions

* How can knowing that you are chosen by God give you confidence?

* Can anything separate us from the love of Christ? How does this passage assure us of His unmovable love?

KID-BUILDER Prayer

Lord, thank You for caring about me.

In Jesus' name. Amen.

Memory Verse:
We know that God makes all things work together for the good of those who love Him and are chosen to be a part of His plan.

Rom. 8:28

Love—The Greatest Gift

I Corinthians 13

Love does not give up. Love is kind. Love is not jealous. Love does not put itself up as being important. Love has no pride. 5Love does not do the wrong thing. Love never thinks of itself. Love does not get angry. Love does not remember the suffering that comes from being hurt by someone. 6Love is not happy with sin. Love is happy with the truth. 7Love takes everything that comes without giving up. Love believes all things. Love hopes for all things. Love keeps on in all things.

8Love never comes to an end. The gift of speaking God's Word will come to an end. The gift of speaking in special sounds will be stopped. The gift of understanding will come to an end. 9For we only know a part now, and we speak only a part. 10When everything is perfect, then we will not need these gifts that are not perfect.

11When I was a child, I spoke like a child. I thought like a child. I understood like a child. Now I am a man. I do not act like a child anymore.

¹²Now that which we see is as if we were looking in a broken mirror. But then we will see everything. Now I know only a part. But then I will know everything in a perfect way. That is how God knows me right now. ¹³And now we have these three: faith and hope and love, but the greatest of these is love.

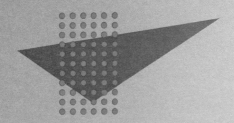

KID-BUILDER Questions

- What does Paul say love is not like?
- According to the truths of this passage, what would you like to change about your way of loving others?
- Why do you think love is greater than faith or hope?

KID-BUILDER Prayer

Lord, I need Your help to love others according to Your Word. *In Jesus' name. Amen.*

Memory Verse:
Love takes everything that comes without giving up. Love believes all things. Love hopes for all things. Love keeps on in all things.

I Cor. 13:7

EPHESIANS

The Whole Armor of God

Ephesians 6

Be strong with the Lord's strength. ¹¹Put on the things God gives you to fight with. Then you will not fall into the traps of the devil. ¹²Our fight is not with people. It is against the leaders and the powers and the spirits of darkness in this world. It is against the demon world that works in the heavens. ¹³Because of this, put on all the things God gives you to fight with. Then you will be able to stand in that sinful day. When it is all over, you will still be standing. ¹⁴So stand up and do not be moved. Wear a belt of truth around your body. Wear a piece of iron over your chest which is being

Kid-Builder Value
DEDICATION is a complete commitment to something or someone. It means that you put your whole heart into what you're doing. Paul is a good example of someone who was dedicated to living for God. He was determined to serve God despite suffering, persecution, and imprisonment. Wearing the armor of God will help equip you to fight any spiritual battles in your walk with God.

right with God. ¹⁵Wear shoes on your feet which are the Good News of peace. ¹⁶Most important of all, you need a covering of faith in front of you. This is to put out the fire-arrows of the devil. ¹⁷The covering for your head is that you have been saved from the punishment of sin. Take the sword of the Spirit which is the Word of God. ¹⁸You must pray at all times as the Holy Spirit leads you to pray. Pray for the things that are needed. You must watch and keep on praying. Remember to pray for all Christians.

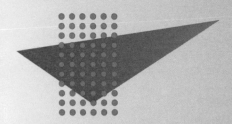

KID-BUILDER Questions

- Name some of the pieces of the armor. Why is each one important?

- Good armor helps boost the courage of its wearer. What do you have that gives you courage? How can the armor of God give you courage?

KID-BUILDER Prayer

Lord, help me put on all the armor and stand up to the attacks of the enemy.   In Jesus' name. Amen.

Memory Verse:
Be strong with the Lord's strength. Put on the things God gives you to fight with.   Eph. 6:10, 11

PHILIPPIANS

The Peace That Comes from God

Philippians 4

Be full of joy always because you belong to the Lord. Again I say, be full of joy! ⁵Let all people see how gentle you are. The Lord is coming again soon. ⁶Do not worry. Learn to pray about everything. Give thanks to God as you ask Him for what you need. ⁷The peace of God is much greater than the human mind can understand. This peace will keep your hearts and minds through Christ Jesus.

⁸Christian brothers, keep your minds thinking about whatever is true, whatever is respected, whatever is right, whatever is pure, whatever can be loved, and whatever is well thought of. If there is anything good and worth giving thanks for, think about these things. ⁹Keep on doing all the things you learned and received and heard from me. Do the things you saw me do. Then the God Who gives peace will be with you. . . . ¹³I can do all things because Christ gives me the strength. . . . ¹⁹And my God will give you everything you need because of His great riches in Christ Jesus.

• •

Kid-Builder Value
SELF-DISCIPLINE is the willingness to correct or control yourself in order to make you a better person. Paul tells us to keep our thoughts on positive godly things.

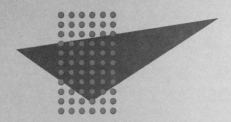

KID-BUILDER Questions

- Read verse 6. How much do you worry? How does worry cancel out discipline? How can the advice in Philippians 4:8 help you not to worry?

- Why is it important to pray about everything? How can a regular time of prayer be a form of discipline?

KID-BUILDER Prayer

Lord, I need help to focus on good thoughts. Lord, thanks for Your help.   *In Jesus' name. Amen.*

Memory Verse:
Christian brothers, keep your minds thinking about whatever is true, whatever is respected, whatever is right, whatever is pure, whatever can be loved, and whatever is well thought of. If there is anything good and worth giving thanks for, think about these things.

Phil. 4:8

COLOSSIANS

You Are God's Chosen

Colossians 3

If then you have been raised with Christ, keep looking for the good things of heaven. This is where Christ is seated on the right side of God. ²Keep your minds thinking about things in heaven. Do not think about things on the earth. ³You are dead to the things of this world. Your new life is now hidden in God through Christ. ⁴Christ is our life. When He comes again, you will also be with Him to share His shining greatness. . . .

⁸Put out of your life these things . . . anger, bad temper, bad feeling toward others, talk that hurts people, speaking against God, and dirty talk. ⁹Do not lie to each other. You have put out of your life your old ways. ¹⁰You have now become a new person and are always learning more about Christ. You are being made more like Christ. He is the One Who made you. ¹¹There is no difference in men in this new life. Greeks and Jews are the same. The man who has gone through the religious act of becoming a Jew and the one who has

not are the same. There is no difference between nations. Men who are sold to work and those who are free are the same. Christ is everything. He is in all of us.

12God has chosen you. You are holy and loved by Him. Because of this, your new life should be full of loving-pity. You should be kind to others and have no pride. Be gentle and be willing to wait for others. 13Try to understand other people. Forgive each other. If you have something against someone, forgive him. That is the way the Lord forgave you. 14And to all these things, you must add love. Love holds everything and everybody together and makes

all these good things perfect. [15]Let the peace of Christ have power over your hearts. You were chosen as a part of His body. Always be thankful.

[16]Let the teaching of Christ and His words keep on living in you. These make your lives rich and full of wisdom. Keep on teaching and helping each other. Sing the Songs of David and the church songs and the songs of heaven with hearts full of thanks to God. [17]Whatever you say or do, do it in the name of the Lord Jesus. Give thanks to God the Father through the Lord Jesus.

Kid-Builder Value
COMMITMENT is a willingness to serve someone or a cause. Jesus wants His people to be committed enough to live lives that are pleasing to God.

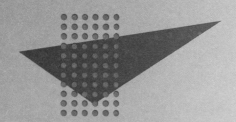

KID-BUILDER Questions

- Why is it important to stop doing things like talking about others in a mean or hurtful way?

- Why is it important to be truthful? How can you demonstrate commitment to Christ by being truthful?

- How can knowing that Jesus is going to return help to influence your behavior? What are some attitudes you have that you think should be changed before He comes back?

KID-BUILDER Prayer

Lord, help me to remember where Jesus is and that He will return for me someday.   In Jesus' name. Amen.

Memory Verse:
Put out of your life these things . . . anger, bad temper, bad feeling toward others, talk that hurts people, speaking against God, and dirty talk.   Col. 3:8

Paul Gives Timothy Advice

II Timothy 1—3

I thank God for you. I pray for you night and day. I am working for God the way my early fathers worked. My heart says I am free from sin. . . . 5I remember your true faith. It is the same faith your grandmother Lois had and your mother Eunice had. I am sure you have that same faith also.

6For this reason, I ask you to keep using the gift God gave you. It came to you when I laid my hands on you and prayed that God would use you. 7For God did not give us a spirit of fear. He gave us a spirit of power and of love and of a good mind. 8Do not be ashamed to tell others about what our Lord said, or of me here in prison. I am here because of Jesus Christ. Be ready to suffer for preaching the Good News and God will give you the strength you need. 9He is the One Who saved us from the punishment of sin. He is the One Who chose us to do His work. It is not because of anything we have done. But it was His plan from the beginning

that He would give us His loving-favor through Christ Jesus. . . .

3:14Hold on to what you have learned and know to be true. Remember where you learned them. 15You have known the Holy Writings since you were a child. They are able to give you wisdom that leads to being saved from the punishment of sin by putting your trust in Christ Jesus. 16All the Holy Writings are God-given and are made alive by Him. Man is helped when he is taught God's Word. It shows what is wrong. It changes the way of a man's life. It shows him how to be right with God. 17It gives the man who belongs to God everything he needs to work well for Him.

Kid-Builder Value
TRUSTWORTHINESS means being worthy of trust. Timothy's godly upbringing helped him be trustworthy.

KID-BUILDER Questions

- What advice did Paul have for Timothy? How could his advice help keep him trustworthy?

- Timothy's role in the church meant that he was trustworthy. Trustworthy people get asked to do important things. What evidence in your life shows others that you are trustworthy?

KID-BUILDER Prayer

Lord, I want to be trusted to do important things. Help me be worthy of trust.

In Jesus' name. Amen.

Memory Verse:
Let no one show little respect for you because you are young. Show other Christians how to live by your life.   I Tim. 4:12

People of Faith

Hebrews 11—12

Now faith is being sure we will get what we hope for. It is being sure of what we cannot see. ²God was pleased with the men who had faith who lived long ago.

³Through faith we understand that the world was made by the Word of God. Things we see were made from what could not be seen. . . .

⁷Because Noah had faith, he built a large boat for his family. God told him what was going to happen. His faith made him hear God speak and he obeyed. His family was saved from death because he built the boat. . . .

⁸Because Abraham had faith, he obeyed God when God called him to leave his home. He was to go to another country that God promised to give him. He left his home without knowing where he was going. . . .

¹¹Because Sarah had faith, she was able to have a child long after she was past the age to have children. She had faith to believe that God would do

what He promised. 12Abraham was too old to have children. But from this one man came a family with as many in it as the stars in the sky and as many as the sand by the sea. . . .

23Because of faith, Moses, after he was born, was hidden by his parents for three months. They saw that he was a beautiful child. They were not afraid of the king when he said that all baby boys should be killed.

24Because Moses had faith, he would not be called the son of Pharaoh's daughter when he grew up. 25He chose to suffer with God's people instead of having fun doing sinful things for awhile. 26Any shame that he suffered for Christ was worth more than all the riches in Egypt. He kept his eyes on the pay God was going to give him. . . .

29Because the Jews had faith, they went through the Red Sea as if they were on dry ground. But when the people of Egypt tried to go through, they were all killed by the water.

30Because the Jews had faith, the walls of the city of Jericho fell down after the Jews had walked around the city for seven days. . . .

Kid-Builder Value
FAITH is the act of believing the things that God has revealed about Himself and acting on those beliefs. Many people in the Bible showed faith in God. This passage in Hebrews celebrates the "Heroes of Faith."

12:1All these many people who have had faith in God are now gathered around watching us. Let us put every thing out of our lives that keeps us from doing what we should. Let us keep running in the race that God has planned for us. 2Let us keep looking to Jesus. Our faith comes from Him and He is the One Who makes it perfect. He did not give up when He had to suffer shame and die on a cross. He knew of the joy that would be His later. Now He is sitting at the right side of God.

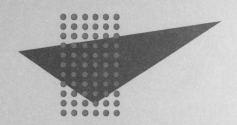

KID-BUILDER Questions

- Name ways each individual showed faith. What do you remember about their stories?

- How did faith in God help them?

- Baseball cards have statistics on each player to show the player's strengths. You've just read the stats of each "hero or heroine of faith." If someone were to make a "baseball card" on your life, what would you want known about your faith?

KID-BUILDER Prayer

Lord, I want to be a hero of faith in my home/ school/neighborhood (pick one).

In Jesus' name. Amen.

Memory Verse:
Now faith is being sure we will get what we hope for. It is being sure of what we cannot see.   Heb. 11:1

• •

Loving Others

I John 3—4

See what great love the Father has for us that He would call us His children. And that is what we are. For this reason the people of the world do not know who we are because they did not know Him. ²Dear friends, we are God's children now. But it has not yet been shown to us what we are going to be. We know that when He comes again, we will be like Him because we will see Him as He is. . . .

¹⁶We know what love is because Christ gave His life for us. We should give our lives for our brothers. ¹⁷What if a person has enough money to live on and sees his brother in need of food and clothing? If he does not help him, how can the love of God be in him? ¹⁸My children, let us not love with words or in talk only. Let us love by what we do and in truth. ¹⁹This is how we know we are Christians. It will give our heart comfort for sure when we stand before Him. . . .

⁴:⁷Dear friends, let us love each other, because

love comes from God. Those who love are God's children and they know God. ⁸Those who do not love do not know God because God is love. ⁹God has shown His love to us by sending His only Son into the world. God did this so we might have life through Christ. ¹⁰This is love! It is not that we loved God but that He loved us. For God sent His Son to pay for our sins with His own blood.

¹¹Dear friends, if God loved us that much, then we should love each other. ¹²No person has ever seen God at any time. If we love each other, God lives in us. ¹³He has given us His Spirit. This is how we live by His help and He lives in us. . . .

¹⁶We have come to know and believe the love God has for us. God is love. If you live in love, you live by the help of God and God lives in you.

¹⁷Love is made perfect in us when we are not ashamed as we stand before Him on the day He says who is guilty. For we know that our life in this world is His life lived in us. ¹⁸There is no fear in love. Perfect love puts fear out of our hearts. People have fear when they are afraid of being punished. The man who is afraid does not have perfect love. ¹⁹We love Him because He loved us first. ²⁰If a person says, "I love God," but hates his brother, he is a liar. If a person does not love his brother whom he has seen, how can he love God Whom he has not seen? ²¹We have these words from Him. If you love God, love your brother also.

Kid-Builder Value
LOVING is more than just a feeling of being attracted to or happy with someone. It includes choosing to be kind and helpful to others even though you may not exactly feel like it. John encouraged Christians to be loving, not just talk about it. Loving others involves actions.

KID-BUILDER Questions

- Where does love come from? How did God show us what love is?

- What are some ways people acted to show love to you?

- How does God help us to love? What are some ways you can show love to others?

KID-BUILDER Prayer

Lord, I want to have an active kind of love that reaches out to help others. I want Your kind of love.

In Jesus' name. Amen.

Memory Verse:
My children, let us not love with words or in talk only. Let us love by what we do and in truth.   I John 3:18

PROPHECY

Prophecy

The last section of the Bible is called *Prophecy*. It contains one book—Revelation (rev-ul-AY-shun). The word *prophecy* means a message from God delivered by a prophet—a man or woman chosen by God. In the Old Testament, we saw how prophets (see Major and Minor Prophets on page 178) were used to tell the Israelites or other people what God had done in the past, what He was doing in the present, and what He would do in the future. The Book of Revelation tells us about God's plan for His family and for those who turn away from Him.

Revelation

John wrote *Revelation* while a captive on the island of Patmos. He was put there as a punishment for his faith in Jesus. While there, God showed John through visions how He is going to defeat sin, remove all evil, and live with His people forever in heaven. Many Scriptures throughout the Bible talk about heaven, but the main description of what it will look like is given to us in the Book of *Revelation*.

REVELATION

The Promise of Heaven

Revelation 21—22

I saw the Holy City, the new Jerusalem. It was coming down out of heaven from God. It was made ready like a bride is made ready for her husband. 3I heard a loud voice coming from heaven. It said, "See! God's home is with men. He will live with them. They will be His people. God Himself will be with them. He will be their God. 4 God will take away all their tears. There will be no more death or sorrow or crying or pain. All the old things have passed away. . . .

10My spirit was carried away by the angel to a very high mountain. He showed me the Holy City of Jerusalem. It was coming out of heaven from God. 11 It was filled with the shining greatness of God. It shone like a stone worth much money, like a jasper stone. It was clear like glass. 12It had a very

Kid-Builder Fact
Rev.21:21 *The Holy City* refers to the place we call *heaven*.

high wall, and there were twelve gates. Twelve angels stood by the gates. The names of the twelve family groups of the Jewish nation were written on the gates....

21The twelve gates were twelve pearls. Each gate was made from one pearl. The street of the city was pure gold. It was as clear as glass.

22 I did not see a house of God in the city. The All-powerful Lord God and the Lamb are the house of God in this city. 23 There is no need for the sun and moon to shine in the city. The shining greatness of God makes it full of light. The Lamb is its light. 24The nations will walk by its light.

The kings of the earth will bring their greatness into it. 25The gates are open all day. They will never be shut. There will be no night there. 26The greatness and honor of all the nations will be brought into it. 27Nothing sinful will go into the city. No one who is sinful-minded or tells lies can go in. Only those whose names are written in the Lamb's book of life can go in. . . .

22:12[Jesus said,] "See! I am coming soon. I am bringing with Me the pay I will give to everyone for what he has done. 13 I am the First and the Last. I am the beginning and the end. 14 Those who wash their clothes clean are happy (who are washed by the blood of the Lamb). . . .

17 The Holy Spirit and the Bride say, "Come!" Let the one who hears say, "Come!" Let the one who is thirsty, come. Let the one who wants to drink of the water of life, drink it. It is a free gift.

18I am telling everyone who hears the words that are written in this book: If anyone adds anything to what is written in this book, God will add to him the kinds of trouble that this book tells about. 19 If anyone takes away any part of this book that tells what will happen in the future, God will take away his part from the tree of life and from the Holy City

Kid-Builder Fact
Rev. 21:27 The Lamb is *Jesus*.

which are written in this book.

²⁰He Who tells these things says, "Yes, I am coming soon!" Let it be so. Come, Lord Jesus. ²¹May all of you have the loving-favor of the Lord Jesus Christ. Let it be so.

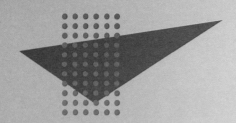

KID-BUILDER Questions

- Have you ever wondered what heaven will be like? How does this passage describe heaven?

- A passage like this was helpful to early Christians who were going through terrible persecution. It gave them something to hope for. When you're facing a bad time, why does it help to look forward to something good?

- The passage talks of Jesus returning. He had promised His followers that He would come again. How can that encourage you to be faithful to Jesus?

KID-BUILDER Prayer

Lord, I want to live with You someday. Help me be faithful to You in the meantime.

In Jesus' name. Amen.

Memory Verse:
God will take away all their tears. There will be no more death or sorrow or crying or pain. All the old things have passed away.

Rev. 21:4

Jesus said,

Do not let your heart be troubled. You have put your trust in God, put your trust in Me also. There are many rooms in My Father's house. If it were not so, I would have told you. I am going away to make a place for you. After I go and make a place for you, I will come back and take you with Me. Then you may be where I am. . . . I am the Way and the Truth and the Life."

John 14:1-3, 6a

• •